MarketABLE

The MVP Asset Recovered

Brittany P. Webb

Edited and assembled in collaboration with ChatGPT by OpenAI. First Edition.
Printed in the United States of America.

eBook: ISBN: 979-8-9994228-4-2
Paperback ISBN: 979-8-9994228-5-9

Dedication

To the woman who carries it all—
the schedules, the feelings, the details, the weight no one sees.
To the one they describe with a half-laugh and a compliment:
"I don't know how she does it."
What they mean is: they've never had to.
To the mother. The wife. The leader. The fixer.
The one who keeps showing up—even when she's tired.
I see you.
This is for you.

Acknowledgements

This book was written in a season that didn't make sense on paper—but it made sense in my spirit. And I didn't get through it alone.

First, thank You, God. For covering what I couldn't control, closing doors that would have cost me my peace, and rebuilding me from the inside out when I thought I was only rebuilding my life. Thank You for quiet strength, daily bread, and the kind of guidance that doesn't always come with a roadmap—just enough light for the next step.

To my family—thank you for your patience as I processed, pivoted, and rebuilt. Thank you for loving me through the messier middle, for giving me room to become, and for reminding me what matters most. You are my grounding, my joy, and my greatest motivation.

To my children—thank you for being my why in the most honest way. You helped me remember that presence matters more than perfection, and that love doesn't have to be loud to be real.

To my friends—thank you for holding space without trying to fix me. Thank you for the prayers, the check-ins, the laughter, the meals, and the steady reminders that I was not alone.

To every woman who has ever carried too much for too long—this book exists because I needed proof that quiet doesn't mean you're behind. It can mean you're becoming. And even if the things you build in certain seasons never go anywhere else in those seasons, your value still stands. Your integrity still counts. Your gifts still remain.

I am still MarketABLE. And you are too.

And to the reader—thank you for trusting me with your time. If these pages help you reclaim your voice, your peace, and your worth, then every word was worth it.

Contents

Preface

Marketable

Marketable *Adjective*. In demand able to be sold, shared, or trusted. In career terms: the kind of person employers want to hire.[1]

For a long time, I was confident, certain, and loyal, until one moment changed it all. I didn't plan an exit strategy. I actually thought if I left one day, that it would be loud and I'd tell them *all the things*. But when words no longer carry weight, walking away was loud enough. Nothing had changed that day, although everything changed all the same. One meeting. Familiar table. One that I figuratively helped build. And I knew what I carried—what I built, what I protected, what I held together. A position can be filled. But presence like that isn't always replaceable. And still, something suddenly shifted in me—my give-a-damn maybe (forgive me, Lord)—like a lightbulb turning on in the dark. My internal shield formed around my character and integrity, knowing I wouldn't be able to honestly do business as usual. Once I see, I can't unsee. So, with that, I maintained composure as I walked out. Of the meeting. Jeez…aren't you jumping the gun?! You're not that far off.

I've never packed so quickly in my life! And I'm a nester. My office is decorated like a second home. Only adrenaline and Jesus were fueling me now! I started secretly packing up my office, loading it into my car, and driving out of that parking lot once more, not to return. I was no longer carrying what wasn't mine to hold. I was free at last. But free, for me came with a cost. The cost. A recommendation. A public endorsement. A polished handoff. I cut ties. Quietly. And for the first time in a long time, I had to face a terrifying thought: *that I might not be marketable.*

Old signatures carry weight—especially on legal agreements. I couldn't explain, correct, or defend myself publicly. I found myself in uncharted waters, trying to keep my head above the waves that rose from my tears, life ahead, and a wild wind of peace that came over me and I left a season in the rear view. So, I did what I had been searching for, and found peace in the silence.

I couldn't really put it into words that made sense, why it felt so hard when I knew it was right. I had been rewarded, affirmed, acknowledged, compensated, and promoted for this consistent, stellar performance, so naturally, I would attach the word marketable to mean productive.

It must mean staying visible. Staying relevant. Staying useful. And proving—quietly—that I still had something to offer. That I hadn't fallen behind. That stepping away wouldn't cost me my place that I had earned, honestly.

I believed marketability was fragile. Something you could lose if you paused too long, chose differently, or let life interrupt the plan.

I thought I was needed. I thought I was useful. I thought you kept it going by continuing to go. Don't we?

Especially as a woman.

Especially in midlife.

Especially after caregiving, health challenges, career shifts, or seasons that didn't translate neatly onto a résumé.

This book is not about how to market yourself.

It's about what happens when you realize that YOU are the MVP asset. And when you feel least Marketable, you have hope in your marketability.

So, realistically, lets reframe Marketable, as I know it now. Marketable, as I use it here, has nothing to do with hustle, optimization, or constant reinvention. It is not a productivity framework or a personal brand strategy. It is a reclaiming of value that exists beneath performance.

Marketable is what remains when the titles fall away.

When the noise quiets.

When you stop reacting and start choosing.

It is clarity.

Self-trust.

Discernment.

The ability to regulate instead of rush, to pause instead of panic, to build—or not build—from alignment rather than fear.

This book was written in a season where much of what once defined me no longer fit. Not because it failed, but because I had outgrown it. What followed was not a dramatic collapse or a polished reinvention—but a slow, honest return to myself.

The chapters that follow trace that return.

Not as a formula.

Not as advice.

But as lived experience—layered with reflection, faith, and hard-earned awareness.

If you are reading this because you feel tired of holding everything together...

If you have wondered whether slowing down means losing ground...

If you sense there is more to your value than what you produce...

This book is not here to tell you who to become.

It is here to remind you of what you already carry.

Read it slowly.

Read it honestly.

Read it without trying to fix yourself.

You are not behind.

You are MarketABLE.

Why This Matters Now

You are not the only one asking the question behind the question.

In a world where roles change fast, organizations pivot without warning, and technology keeps rewriting the rules, it is easy to let your worth feel conditional.

This book is here to pull your value out of the hands of outcomes - and put it back where it belongs: in your clarity, your character, your discernment, and your ability to rebuild without abandoning yourself.

If you are navigating any of this, you are in the right place:

• a career shift you did not choose

• a season where you cannot share the whole story

• financial pressure that makes you want to rush

• a body that is tired of living on adrenaline

• the fear that AI, culture, or the economy will outrun what you are building or run it over altogether

This is not a productivity book in disguise. It is a reclamation book. A return to your internal proof - so that external validation becomes a bonus, not a requirement.

The Month It Clicked

Even as I began to understand that worth is deeper than output, I still reached for productivity when I felt afraid. Motion had always been my comfort. If I could make something happen, I could calm the uncertainty inside me—at least for a moment.

Then the holidays came, and for the first time in a long time, I let myself stop without immediately replacing the silence with a new plan.

I sat for a month—really sat. Something I hadn't ever given myself. Let's be realistic, who actually can afford to sit for a month. Well, when you don't have a choice but to, after filling 18 months before with everything you could think of to create movement and momentum, and it comes to a slow roll, you get it by default, rather than choice, necessarily. Although, I chose to see it as a gift. After a long season of emotional work, and steady building, I decided to be intentional and soaked up the ordinary moments that I used to rush past: a slow cup of coffee in a quiet house, with the twinkle of the warm white Christmas lights that sparkled around our nostalgic, traditional ornaments that adorned our fresh pine tree we pick out each year as a family, one of our favorite traditions. The smell of Christmas, laughter from the next room, the rhythm of meals and family visits, shopping, wrapping, and driving around town gazing at the impressive display of Christmas lights and bag lights and candlelight church services, rich routines that never make it onto a résumé but somehow hold an entire life together, over a month of creating memories in what for most is the "most wonderful time of the year", and one I have admittedly rushed through for way too many years. But this year, it resonated on a whole other level.

Present. Awake. Aware. Healed. Grateful. Unwilling to rush what seemed clear before and now, uncertain in the quiet. And so, this season became yet another, when I asked what to do with the waiting. And the answer was simple: Build a chair. Have a seat. Stay a while. Observe and Participate. Don't just stand at the door waiting. Take it all in, and the answers will come. In due time.

At one point, I typed a line that stopped me cold: Maybe you don't earn peace. Maybe you receive it. Peace is a funny thing. God gives us peace, and just like prayer, when we give it to God, we are supposed to let Him handle it. But, I like control, or think I do, so I take things back into my own hands and ironically, that's the same things that takes my peace away. So it becomes a dance, and one I enjoy sitting out and soaking in the peace while I release and receive it.

During this season, I wasn't creating as much content at the capacity as I was previously; I was paying attention, with the new-found down-time. And paying attention was the first step to remembering who I was - and who I was becoming.

Flowers blooming in odd corners of the yard. Leaves falling from the trees. Crisp, cool air in the sky. A plant by the window that soaked up the one ray of light at 11am that snuck in past our wrap-around porch . A single sentence in my journal that felt like oxygen.

I started noticing small things again - not to document them, but to let them regulate me.

And in that slower pace, the questions I had been outrunning finally caught up to me.

What if my app doesn't build the way I originally planned?

What if AI advances faster than I can anticipate, and Prompt Therapy™ becomes outdated before it ever has the chance to stand on its own?

What if the business I started out to build, with the frameworks I created, wasn't the end goal?

What if the ideas I'm carrying never become what I hoped—and I don't do anything else with any of it?

Then the question underneath all the other questions surfaced, plain and unprotected:

Am I still marketable? Did any of it matter?

I expected my mind to argue. I expected the familiar panic to rise and demand proof. But in the quiet, the answer arrived without effort.

Yes.

Not because I had a perfect plan. Not because I could predict the market. Not because I was producing enough to justify my place in the world. The answer was yes because my value was never owned by the outcome of my work. I had built it in a season of alignment and faith-led purpose. It was never dependent on how quickly something shipped, how many people approved, or how impressive the next step looked from the outside.

I realized I had spent years believing that my security lived on the other side of execution. But during that month of pause, I felt a different kind of security—one still rooted in alignment and faith, but also with the simple truth that capability doesn't disappear when the calendar slows down, the doors that once opened freely now seem to close with uncertainty, and realization that I am still excited about what is ahead, whatever that may be. And it wasn't for nothing. I grew. I learned. I danced. I lived. I repaired cracks in my foundation and celebrate every little thing I experienced intentionally. And confidently, clearly, and loyally voiced an affirmation, "You're going to be okay. Better than okay. You're ready. Come what may."

And then, as if to underline what I had just learned, something small happened that I didn't see coming.

It wasn't the thing that made me marketable. It was simply a mirror that reflected what I had finally accepted: I was internally marketable—and yes, I could be externally validated too.

I didn't need that panel to tell me who I was or to be true to myself. I had already secured that for myself. So, instead, I received it as a gentle confirmation that I was on the right path. Aligned. Ready for whatever comes my way. And the pieces that it showcased, were exactly who I am. It is me, and I am proud of my story, internally and externally.

If you're reading this in a season of uncertainty, I want you to know something: the pause is not a threat. Sometimes the pause is where the answer finds you. When you finally start trying so hard to find it.

Hold This

Your marketability is not fragile. It is not cancelled by uncertainty. It is carried in the parts of you that remain when outcomes change.

Try This

- What would it look like to let peace be evidence, not a reward?
- What am I afraid will become 'obsolete' - and what does that fear reveal about what I think I am worth?
- Where am I treating my value like it has an expiration date?

Practice for seven days: Choose one moment per day to pause on purpose (no fixing, no planning) and name what you notice in your body. End with one sentence: 'The truth I can carry today is _____.'

What This Book Will Do for You

This is a reclaiming book. It is designed to help you recover your value when a role, season, or system tried to redefine it.

By the end, you should be able to:

- Name the exact lie you learned about worth (and where you learned it).
- Separate your value from your output without losing your ambition.
- Set boundaries that protect your peace without becoming hard.
- Make decisions from alignment instead of urgency or fear.
- Put language to your identity shift so you can talk about it with confidence (in life, work, and relationships).

The MarketABLE Method

If you want a simple way to apply this book instead of only reflecting on it, use these five shifts. They are not hustle steps. They are worth steps.

PAUSE: Stop proving. Slow the nervous system. Make space for truth to surface.

NAME: Name what happened without over-explaining. Name what you lost, and what you learned.

RECLAIM: Reclaim what is true about you: character, capability, faith, discernment, and voice.

REALIGN: Realign your time, boundaries, and commitments around what matters most in this season.

REBUILD: Rebuild forward from peace - not panic. Create the next version of your life on purpose.

How to Read This Book

You can read it straight through, but it works best when you let it meet you slowly. If a chapter stings, pause. If a paragraph feels like relief, underline it. The goal is not to finish quickly - the goal is to come back to yourself.

If you are using this in a transition season, try this rhythm:

- Read one chapter.
- Write one sentence: "The lie I have been living is…"

- Write one sentence: "The truth I am choosing is…"
- Choose one boundary or decision to practice for seven days.

The MarketABLE Strategy

This book offers a simple strategy for reclaiming your sense of value—because healing usually moves in stages, even when life feels chaotic.

- Unraveling → when the old proof stops working and you feel exposed.
- Recalibration → when you stop chasing momentum and start listening for truth.
- Reclaiming → when you rebuild your inner definition of value (quiet, solid, portable).
- Reentry → when you move forward again from alignment—not adrenaline.

You may recognize yourself in more than one stage at a time. That's normal. Let the chapters meet you where you are—and trust the progression.

Your MarketABLE Signature

If you're reading this, you likely already have a strong, identifiable throughline—a consistent strength that shows up in your work, your home, your relationships, and the way you handle pressure. This may be your unique wiring and the very thing that makes you *you*—your MarketABLE Signature.

We honor that. We celebrate it. This book is not here to change who you are. It's here to help you recognize the patterns that may no longer be healthy fuel. Under prolonged pressure, even your greatest strengths can start to distort—when proving takes over, urgency replaces alignment, and strength becomes survival at the cost of peace.

As you read, you'll learn how to keep your signature intact while shifting patterns that drain you. That's how you reclaim your worth without losing your edge—no matter what changes outside you. Your MarketABLE Signature is worth protecting, and I'll show you how.

If You Only Remember One Page

These are the sentences I want repeating in your head when you walk into a room, an interview, a hard conversation, or a quiet morning where you feel behind.

- I am not behind - I am rebuilding.
- I do not have to be constantly useful to be worthy.
- My integrity is not negotiable, even when it costs me.
- Peace is not laziness. It is alignment.
- I can be ambitious without abandoning myself.
- Boundaries are not rejection. They are clarity.
- I can grieve what I lost and still trust what God is doing.
- I do not owe anyone a version of me that requires self-erasure.
- I am allowed to change my mind, my pace, and my path.
- I am marketABLE: VALUEable, LOVEable, and capABLE of what comes.

Book Club and Discussion Guide

If you read this with friends or a women's group, use these prompts to start honest conversation:

- Where did you learn that being needed equals being valuable?
- What is one way "strength" became an expectation in your life?
- What boundary would protect your peace right now - and what fear keeps you from setting it?
- What part of your identity feels most threatened in a transition season?
- What does "marketABLE" mean to you after reading this?
- What would change if you measured your life by alignment instead of productivity?
- What is one next step you will take this week as an act of self-trust?

[1] "Marketable." Vocabulary.com Dictionary, Vocabulary.com, accessed January 4, 2026.

Introduction

When I Stopped, My Life Didn't Fall Apart

My life didn't fall apart when I stopped.

That was the fear—that if I slowed down, said no, or stepped back, everything I had worked so hard to hold together would unravel. That the wheels would come off. That people would be disappointed. That the structure I had spent years supporting would collapse under its own weight. And while I cared deeply, it mattered greatly. But when it appeared my care was greater than theirs, I chose to take care of me, for once.

And stepped out, back, whatever you want to call it. I quit. And for a while, I can only imagine that it did look like things were falling apart.

Not for me—for me, it looked like space I created to put the pieces I freely gave away, stayed with me, in fragile state, but repairable. For them, and the systems and rhythms that had relied on my constant motion, they didn't have me to run it and I can speculate that "replacement" wasn't an option without restructuring, reassessment, and reinforcements to manage the responsibilities I once sacrificed for. The wheels I had been keeping on for my sanity to keep rolling, suddenly came loose, without the weight of their needs to keep it weighted-down and running as it had for so long now, and from the outside it may have looked like breakdown.

But what actually happened was a change in shape.

The parts didn't shatter. They reorganized. What once rolled forward only because I kept driving and pushing learned how to move differently. It turns out that when something stops carrying what it's not meant to carry any longer, it doesn't always crash. Sometimes it becomes lighter. Sometimes it finds air…and soars freely among the clouds!

What may have felt like loss to others, felt like space to me.

And in that space, I didn't fall apart. I came together.

Not all at once. Not dramatically. But through intentional choices made day by day, moment by moment. Through deciding to stop filling every waking hour with other people's direction, needs, plans, and expectations. Through reclaiming my time—not as a rebellion, but as a responsibility.

I didn't stop caring.

I stopped over-functioning.

I didn't stop loving.

I stopped abandoning myself.

For a long time, I believed that being needed was the same as being valuable. That saying yes was proof of commitment. That endurance was the measure of strength and dedication. And I was very good at it—holding everything, managing everything, making it work no matter the cost.

Until I realized the cost was me.

So I made a decision—not to overhaul my life, but to take ownership of it.

I began asking a different question each day: Does this bring me closer to who I'm becoming, or further away from myself?

I started saying no to what no longer served my soul—not in anger, not in defiance, but in honesty. And I started saying yes to what brought me closer to a steadier, more intentional happiness. Not the loud kind. The lasting kind.

The kind rooted in peace.

Nothing broke when I stopped.

What broke was the belief that I had to carry everything to be worthy of what I had.

And in the space that opened, where exhaustion used to live, I found clarity, strength, and a deeper sense of alignment than I had ever known.

This book is about that space.

About what happens when a woman who has always shown up decides to show up for herself.

You are never starting from zero again.

Hold This

Stopping does not mean you are failing. Sometimes stopping is the first act of alignment.

Try This

- What is one thing I could release this week without consequences?
- What part of me is tired of being 'the reliable one'?
- What am I afraid will fall apart if I stop performing?

Practice: Pick one small 'non-essential yes' and turn it into a kind no. Notice what happens - not externally, internally.

Chapter 1
The Woman Who Holds Everything

"If I can be hired, I can be healed—and I can be honest about both."
— Brittany P. Webb

There is a woman everyone relies on.

She is capable, dependable, steady. She notices what needs to be done before anyone asks. She remembers the schedules, carries the conversations, manages the logistics, and absorbs the emotional weight of the room without announcing it.

People say, "I don't know how she does it."

What they mean is: They've never had to.

This woman does not collapse when things get hard. She adjusts. She absorbs. She adapts. And because she can, she does—again and again—until strength is no longer something she chooses, but something that is expected of her.

Sociologists call this invisible labor. Psychologists call it emotional load. Scripture simply calls it being weary.

"Come to me, all you who are weary and burdened, and I will give you rest."

—Matthew 11:28

What's striking about that verse is not the invitation to rest—but the assumption. You are already burdened. The weariness is acknowledged, not questioned.

Yet many women live as if rest must be earned.

Strength becomes a quiet contract: If I can carry it, I should.

Competence becomes obligation: If I do it well, it becomes mine to keep doing.

Over time, this creates a dangerous misunderstanding—that holding everything is proof of worth.

Author and researcher Brené Brown writes that "perfectionism is not the same thing as striving to be your best. Perfectionism is a shield." For many women, strength functions the same way. It protects. It produces. And it hides how much is being carried.

The woman who holds everything rarely announces when the load gets heavy. She has learned how to move forward even when she is tired, disappointed, or unsure. She does not wait for ideal conditions. She makes things work.

And the world rewards her for it.

Workplaces promote her reliability. Families depend on her stability. Communities lean on her consistency. Faith traditions praise her service.

But no one asks what it costs her.

Scripture warns gently but clearly:

"Better one handful with tranquility than two handfuls with toil and chasing after the wind."

—Ecclesiastes 4:6

Still, many women believe that peace is something to pursue later—after the season passes, after the crisis resolves, after the needs lessen. They live as if this pace is temporary, even when years pass and nothing slows.

I lived inside that belief for a long time.

Not because I didn't love my life—but because I didn't know another way to carry it myself. What I really wanted was to carry it—with intention, faith, and courage—without disappearing from the life I love.

The woman who holds everything rarely sets out to do so.

She becomes her out of necessity, expectation, and quiet competence. Somewhere along the way, she notices that she is the one who fills the gaps—emotionally, logistically, spiritually. If something needs to be remembered, carried, smoothed over, or done well, it often lands in her hands.

Not because she asked for it.

Because she could.

Over time, this creates an unspoken agreement: If I can handle it, I will.

And if she doesn't? Things feel unstable.

This is how strength slowly shifts from a virtue into a requirement.

She learns to anticipate before being asked. She absorbs disappointment without naming it. She keeps moving even when her body and spirit are asking for pause. And because she doesn't collapse, no one questions the load.

The world has language for this now. We talk about burnout, invisible labor, emotional load. But long before there were studies or hashtags, there was simply a woman doing what needed to be done—again and again—without space to ask whether it was sustainable.

Scripture never mistakes endurance for holiness.

"Better one handful with tranquility than two handfuls with toil and chasing after the wind."

—Ecclesiastes 4:6

Yet many women live as though peace is a reward they will earn later—after the season ends, after the crisis passes, after the needs lessen. They tell themselves this is temporary, even as years accumulate and nothing truly slows.

I once wrote, "I wasn't lost. I was between definitions."

At the time, I meant it professionally. Now I understand it more personally.

So many women are not failing—they are simply living inside definitions that no longer fit.

The definition of a good mother.

A strong partner.

A reliable leader.

A faithful woman.

A capable professional.

Each definition, on its own, may be meaningful. But stacked together without reflection, they become heavy. And eventually, something inside begins to ask a quieter question—not Can I keep going? but Should I?

This is where the tension begins.

Because the woman who holds everything does not want to stop loving, supporting, or showing up. She does not want to abandon her family, her faith, her work, or her commitments. What she wants—often without fully realizing it—is to stop disappearing inside them.

There is a difference.

Psalm 23 speaks of restoration, not replacement.

"He restores my soul."

Not my résumé.

Not my output.

Not my usefulness.

My soul.

Restoration does not require erasing your life. It requires reordering it.

For me, this realization came slowly. Not in a single moment of collapse, but in the accumulation of small recognitions. I noticed how often I said yes out of habit rather than alignment. How easily my time filled with other people's priorities. How rarely I asked myself whether a choice brought me closer to who I was becoming—or further away.

When I stopped long enough to notice, it was uncomfortable.

Marketable

Not because everything was wrong—but because everything had been running on momentum.

For a while, the disruption unsettled the systems around me. Things changed shape. Expectations adjusted. The wheels I had been keeping on loosened, and it looked—briefly—like loss.

But what followed was not ruin. It was space.

Space to choose intentionally instead of reactively.

Space to say no without apology.

Space to say yes without resentment.

What I learned is this: when a woman who has been holding everything pauses, the world does not end. It reorganizes.

And often, it finds new ways to move.

This is the part that surprises most women. We are taught to believe that our constant motion is what keeps everything together. That if we stop, everything will fall apart. But what often falls away instead is what was never meant to be carried by us alone.

Isaiah writes in Isaiah 30:15, "In quietness and trust is your strength."

Quietness is not absence.

It is intention.

Trust is not passivity.

It is discernment.

The woman who holds everything does not need to become someone else. She does not need to harden, withdraw, or disappear. She needs permission, often self-given, to remain present without being consumed.

That permission changes how she lives.

She still shows up.

She still loves deeply.

She still carries responsibility.

But she no longer confuses exhaustion with faithfulness, or self-erasure with strength.

And that is where everything begins to shift.

What surprised me most was not that my life became quieter when I stopped—but that it became clearer.

Without the constant hum of obligation, patterns emerged. I could see which commitments were life-giving and which were merely familiar. I noticed how often I had confused urgency with importance, and service with self-sacrifice. I began to understand that just because I could carry something didn't mean it was mine to hold.

Clarity has a way of rearranging things.

Some expectations softened. Some rhythms changed. Some conversations became more honest. And while not everything adjusted easily, what remained felt truer—more aligned with who I was becoming rather than who I had been trying to sustain.

This kind of clarity does not come from quitting life. It comes from entering it more deliberately.

I once wrote, "Honesty was enough to open the door."

What I understand now is that honesty is also what keeps the door from closing again.

Honesty about limits.

Honesty about desire.

Honesty about what peace requires.

Scripture offers a quiet reminder that still resonates deeply with me:

"Teach us to number our days, that we may gain a heart of wisdom." — Psalm 90:12

Wisdom is not found in doing more. It is found in discerning what matters now. In recognizing seasons. In honoring capacity. In choosing presence over performance.

When a woman who has always shown up begins to live this way, she does not become less dependable. She becomes more rooted. She still contributes, still loves, still leads—but from a place that no longer demands her disappearance as the price of belonging.

This is not a story about walking away.

It is a story about coming back.

Coming back to one's body.

To one's breath.

To one's values.

To one's faith.

Coming back to the quiet truth that a life well-lived does not require constant proof.

The woman who holds everything does not need permission from the world to set things down. But she often needs permission from herself—to believe that doing so will not undo what she loves.

It won't.

What falls away is what was never meant to define her.

What remains is steadier, truer, and strong enough to last.

Marketable

This chapter is an invitation—not to change everything at once, but to notice. To pause. To ask gentler, braver questions. To begin paying attention to where strength has quietly turned into strain, and where peace has been postponed without reason.

In the chapters that follow, we will explore how women come to hold so much, why it becomes expected, and how reclaiming oneself does not require abandoning the life one has built.

It requires intention.

And that is where the work—and the healing—truly begins.

You are never starting from zero again.

Hold This

Strength is not your identity. It is a season, a skill, and sometimes a shield. Your worth was never meant to be proven by how much you can carry.

Try This

- What am I holding that no one has asked me to hold?
- Where have I confused being dependable with being responsible for everyone's peace?
- What would it look like to set down one invisible load this week?

Practice: Write down the top three things you 'always' manage. Circle one. Ask, delegate, delay, or delete - just one.

Chapter 2
The Woman Who Keeps Everything Moving

"The math changed when I stopped measuring worth by output."
— Brittany P. Webb

My kids went to school.

My husband went to work.

No one would know.

There were no visible signs that anything was off. No interruptions to the rhythm of our days. The house emptied the way it always had. Backpacks packed. Cars pulled out of the driveway. Life continued on schedule.

From the outside, everything was fine.

And in many ways, it was.

I got up each morning. I got dressed. I made a pot of coffee and sat with it slowly, intentionally, sipping it hot from one of my favorite mugs. I have many. I didn't rush the morning, but I didn't hide from it either. I created space to be awake to the day—even when I didn't yet know what the day would ask of me.

It would have been easy not to.

It would have been easy to stay in pajamas. To crawl back into bed. To let the hours blur together the way they once had in earlier seasons—those stay-at-home-mom years when exhaustion ran so deep that some days, in the early newborn months especially, I changed from one set of pajamas into another, unsure what day it was, dog tired and running on instinct alone.

I had lived that kind of depletion before.

This was different.

I was awake. Alert. Functioning. Present. Ready.

Even without clarity.

Even without a plan.

I wasn't avoiding life. I was meeting it intentionally.

The quiet truth is this: many women don't fall apart when things get hard. They tighten their grip. They keep the wheels turning. They maintain the rhythms that keep everyone else steady—especially when the inside work is heavy.

Functioning becomes camouflage.

Marketable

No one asks questions when the kids are cared for, the marriage is intact, and the calendar keeps moving. No one checks on the woman who shows up, gets dressed, and keeps going—because from the outside, she looks fine.

But "fine" is not the same as whole.

And choosing to show up doesn't mean nothing is happening beneath the surface.

Sometimes it means the opposite. That everything is happening beneath the surface.

Looking fine protected me—from myself.

It protected me from having to admit, even internally, that something wasn't right. If I looked steady, functional, put together, then my body and my mind didn't have to receive a different message. I could keep going. I could keep managing. I could keep the discomfort contained.

For years, my body told a different story anyway.

I lived with ulcerative colitis that started in my late 20's and with that, the gift of regular colonoscopies, if you've never had one, you're not missing anything. Actually, that's a dream, no really, they call it twilight, some good stuff right there, compared to the prep it requires. In addition to the joys of precautionary procedures, the unpredictable rhythm of stress-related flareups, and the management said stress thereof was quite a feat in and of itself. The anxiety about the flareup became part of the cycle—the fear of it was often enough to bring it on. My body responded to what my mind was holding, whether I acknowledged it or not.

When I was placed on anti-anxiety medication, something unexpected happened: the flareups stopped.

That was the moment I could no longer pretend this was coincidence.

My doctor said something simple and unsettling: You can't hide things from your body. You can't convince it you're fine when you're not. You can't bypass stress by ignoring it. The body listens—to what the mind rehearses, to what the nervous system believes, to what we allow ourselves to feel.

He told me that what my body needed wasn't more control—it was rest. Safety. An internal environment that allowed my mind to stand down from constant vigilance.

Eventually, the body would follow. I spent years on the medication. Eventually, my body healed, and I've been in remission from UC since 2019, and completely off the medicine since 2023.

But that idea my doctor shared with me years ago, echoed something I had heard my entire life in a different language.

Scripture doesn't say try harder not to worry.

It says, do not worry—again and again.

Not as a rebuke, but as an invitation.

Worry is not a fault, but rather a signal. A sign that the mind is trying to protect us by staying alert, rehearsing outcomes, scanning for risk. For someone wired like me—an overthinker, an external processor, deeply empathetic and emotionally attuned—that vigilance came naturally.

But vigilance is not the same as safety.

Over time, I learned that my body needed me to create conditions where my mind could rest. That meant cultivating a positive mindset not as denial, but as discipline. Gratitude not as platitude, but as practice. Habits not as rules, but as scaffolding for steadiness.

Especially in seasons of uncertainty.

Especially during transition.

Especially when clarity was still forming.

Looking fine had kept everything moving.

But learning to be honest—with my body, my mind, and my faith—allowed healing to begin.

This wasn't about fixing myself.

It was about listening.

Outside of my active reflection time—where emotions surfaced freely and sometimes loudly—I needed something steadier to return to.

So I created a simple practice.

Each day, sometimes once, sometimes more than once, I sat with my journal and wrote a short list of truths. Eight or ten if I could find them. Fewer if that's all the day allowed.

They weren't affirmations in the performative sense. They weren't wishes. They were anchors—things I could identify as true even when my emotions were spiraling.

I am a kind-hearted person.

I am good at creating warm and inviting spaces.

I am truly loved by God, my family, and my friends.

I am really good at problem-solving.

I tend to get myself in trouble when I don't set firm boundaries.

Some days the truths were gentle.

Some days they were corrective.

What mattered was that they were honest.

Marketable

This wasn't about convincing myself of something new. It was about reminding myself of what had always been there—beneath the noise, beneath the fear, beneath the urge to manage everything at once.

When my mind raced ahead, this practice brought me back. When uncertainty made everything feel fragile, these truths grounded me in what was stable. They gave my nervous system something solid to rest against. Not the why, but the who.

The grounding who of my being, that I know to be true.

Scripture speaks often about renewal of the mind—not as a one-time event, but as a daily posture.

"Be transformed by the renewing of your mind."

—Romans 12:2

Renewal, I learned, does not happen by suppressing emotion. It happens by creating space for truth to coexist with it.

I could be anxious and kind.

Uncertain and capable.

Tired and deeply loved.

Naming these truths didn't erase the challenges I was facing—but it changed how I met them. Instead of spiraling outward, I learned to orient inward. Instead of rehearsing worst-case scenarios, I practiced returning to what was already known. Naming truths. Naming Feelings. And deciphering between things that stay and things that are transient, seasonal, and short-lived.

This was not toxic positivity.

It was discernment.

It was practice. It was emotional intelligence exercises during my reflective processing I practiced often.

It was choosing not to let my most anxious thoughts become the loudest authority in the room. And recognizing when it didn't deserve energy or time, as it would soon lose its importance and space it was trying to hold in my head and even my heart.

Over time, these small, intentional moments accumulated. They didn't make life easier—but they made it steadier. And steadiness, I discovered, is what allows a woman to keep showing up without losing herself.

Boundaries became clearer. Habits became kinder. My mind learned, slowly, that it did not need to stay on high alert to keep me safe.

Truth was doing that now.

Truth has a way of making boundaries unavoidable.

Once I began naming what was true—about my capacity, my patterns, my limits—it became impossible to keep living as if nothing needed to change. Some boundaries emerged naturally. Others required intention. All of them required courage.

And not everyone welcomed them.

When people are used to your yes, your no feels like a disruption. When you've been agreeable, flexible, and accommodating—when you've learned to smooth edges and keep the peace—any shift can feel, to others, like withdrawal or resistance.

It isn't.

It's reorientation.

But reorientation is uncomfortable for systems and relationships that have relied on your compliance. Work environments accustomed to your availability may push back. Personal relationships that benefited from your overextension may question the change. Some people will interpret your boundaries not as care for yourself, but as inconvenience to them.

This is where many women falter—not because the boundary is wrong, but because the reaction is hard.

We are taught, subtly and repeatedly, that being agreeable is a virtue. That keeping everyone happy is a form of kindness. That rocking the boat is a failure of character rather than a sign of growth.

So when boundaries are met with tension instead of applause, doubt creeps in.

Am I being selfish?

Am I overreacting?

Is this worth the discomfort?

It is.

Because boundaries are not walls.

They are clarity.

They are not punishment.

They are protection.

They are not rejection.

They are honesty.

Marketable

Scripture reminds us that even Jesus did not meet every demand placed on Him. He withdrew. He rested. He said no. Not because He lacked compassion—but because He understood calling and capacity.

There will be moments when setting a boundary costs you approval. There may be relationships that need to adjust—or, in some cases, loosen their grip. That doesn't mean you are doing something wrong. It means the relationship is recalibrating around a truer version of you.

And that recalibration, though uncomfortable, is often necessary.

What I learned is this: the pushback doesn't last forever. What lasts is the peace that follows. The steadiness. The ability to show up without resentment. The freedom to give from a place that isn't depleted.

Boundaries change the tone of your life.

They make room for intention.

They protect the truths you've named.

They allow your yes to mean something again.

And though the adjustment may not be easy, it is worth it—every time.

For a long time, I believed I had to respond to everything.

Every misunderstanding.

Every tension.

Every emotion—mine or someone else's.

If something upset me, I gave it my energy. If someone was frustrated, I felt responsible to explain, clarify, fix, or smooth it over. Silence felt irresponsible. Pause felt like avoidance. Restraint felt like weakness.

I didn't yet understand how much power I was handing away.

There is a scene in the movie War Room that stayed with me long after the credits rolled—the idea of taking battles out of your own hands and placing them somewhere higher. Of letting God fight what you were never meant to carry alone.

That kind of trust is harder than it sounds.

Because it takes strength not to speak.

It takes discipline not to react.

It takes patience not to see results right when you ask.

And it takes maturity not to insist on the last word.

Someone on a podcast I caught while scrolling said that the person who needs the final word loses. At first, that felt backward to me. In the middle of an argument, having the last word feels like control. Like victory.

But control is not the same as strength.

Strength is knowing when not to engage.

When to let them fill the space with truths that may reveal things to you that you wouldn't have gotten had you spoken last.

Practicing the pause—during disagreements, boundary setting, or emotional intensity—became one of the most challenging lessons of my life. And also one of the most freeing.

I remember a visual my husband shared with me years ago, when I was newly out of college and driving our newborn baby around. He explained what to do if the car began to hydroplane: whatever you do, don't slam on the brakes. That only causes the car to spin. Instead, take your foot off the pedals and let the weight of the vehicle slow itself down.

That image stayed with me. And made sense.

Over time, it became a metaphor for my thoughts—and my reactions.

I realized that the more I tried to fix things, add context, explain myself, or make a situation different, the more energy I gave it. The motion increased. The anxiety amplified. The problem grew louder.

Where other parties were included, it would seem to drag them into the situation deeper, emotions heightened, activated, and stirred-up—spinning.

But when I paused, and stepped out of the driver's seat I had placed myself in, and probably didn't belong—the opposite happened.

The situation lost momentum.

The energy softened.

The noise diminished.

Sometimes, it stopped altogether.

This wasn't passivity.

It was wisdom.

Restraint doesn't mean you don't care. It means you care enough not to escalate what doesn't require your control. It means trusting that not every thought needs to be followed, not every emotion needs to be acted on, and not every situation needs your immediate response.

Letting go of the need to manage everything felt risky at first. But what I found on the other side was peace—the kind that comes from knowing you don't have to carry every outcome.

When I paused, gave space, and allowed things to unfold without my constant intervention, problems often lost their power. They slowed. They shifted. They passed.

Like a storm that blows over once you stop trying to drive through it.

Marketable

And in that stillness, I learned something essential:

strength isn't found in reaction—it's found in restraint.

When I stopped reacting to everything around me, something unexpected happened.

The constant anticipation of conflict began to fade.

I hadn't realized how much energy I was spending predicting tension—reading between lines that weren't there, assigning meaning before context arrived, bracing myself for outcomes that hadn't happened yet. My mind stayed one step ahead, rehearsing conversations, imagining reactions, preparing defenses, protecting myself from imaginary threats.

Silence used to feel dangerous.

It felt like something I needed to fill—with words, explanations, action, anything. The quiet felt awkward, exposed, uncomfortable. I mistook it for punishment rather than peace.

But slowly, that changed.

I learned that silence doesn't demand resolution. It offers space. And space allows clarity to arrive on its own.

I stopped predicting outcomes I had no real information for. I stopped writing stories in my head and then reacting as if they were already true. I began to notice how often my assumptions leaned toward the worst-case scenario—not because it was likely, but because it felt protective.

My mom says to us all, often, "If you're going to make up a story in your head, why not make up a good one?"

It was simple advice—Momma Knows Best—but it took me years to understand its depth.

As a chronic overthinker, I believed I was good at predicting outcomes. And sometimes, I probably was, receiving affirmation and encouragement to continue my Pink Panther private investigator degree with Inspector Clouseau. Obviously not a thing but proves my point. Some of those instincts were trauma responses—learned vigilance that once kept me safe. But I've come to see that other times, I may have, and sometimes likely and unknowingly created the very scenarios I feared most.

By bracing for the worst, I rehearsed it.

By expecting disappointment, I shaped my posture toward it.

By speaking fear aloud, I gave it weight.

I told myself it was protection—that if I expected the worst, I wouldn't be blindsided. That I wouldn't be devastated. That I could say, I saw this coming.

But in hindsight, most of the stories I told myself never came true.

I spent so much time conjuring drama and gloomy outcomes in the name of self-protection—only to discover how often I was wrong. And how much life I missed while waiting for things to fall apart.

Now, I know better.

The likelihood that I truly know what will happen next is far lower than I once believed. More often than not, I've been surprised—in good ways, in unexpected ways, in ways that reminded me I am not the author of every outcome.

So I choose differently now.

If a story must be written in my mind, I let it lean toward hope. If an outcome is unknown, I let it remain open. And most importantly, I pray about it more than I think about it or talk about it.

That shift changed everything.

Prayer doesn't guarantee a specific result—but it reorders the heart. It replaces rumination with trust. It moves the burden from my mind to a place it was always meant to rest.

If something doesn't come to pass, I no longer assume loss. I trust that God is protecting me from what isn't meant for me—at least not now. And if it does come to pass, then we rejoice, we celebrate, and we figure it out together.

Either way, there is peace in having an answer.

The woman who keeps everything moving doesn't need to predict every turn. She doesn't need to fill every silence. She doesn't need to anticipate every conflict to be prepared.

Sometimes, the strongest thing she can do is pause.

Sometimes, the wisest thing she can do is trust.

And sometimes, the bravest thing she can do is let the story unfold without trying to write the ending herself.

That is not surrender.

That is faith in motion.

You are never starting from zero again.

Hold This

Keeping everything moving is not the same as keeping yourself alive. You don't have to run at full speed to be faithful, loving, or effective.

Try This

Marketable

- Where do I rush because I'm afraid of what happens if I slow down?
- What have I been calling 'normal' that is actually chronic pressure?
- What is one small boundary that would create breathing room?

Practice: Add a 10-minute buffer before one commitment this week. Treat it as non-negotiable.

Chapter 3
When Strength Becomes the Expectation

"Sometimes the table isn't the problem; it's what you're asked to ignore at it."
— Brittany P. Webb

Strength is a gift—until it becomes a role.

Most women don't volunteer to be "the strong one." They grow into it slowly, through competence, care, and consistency. They are the ones who step in when something needs to be done, who notice what others miss, who hold things together when uncertainty presses in.

At first, strength is recognized. Appreciated. Even admired.

But over time, something subtle shifts.

What was once praised becomes presumed.

What was once help becomes habit.

What was once offered becomes expected.

And because the strong woman rarely complains, rarely collapses, rarely asks for rescue, no one thinks to question the weight she's carrying. Her capacity becomes the baseline. Her steadiness becomes the standard.

She becomes reliable in ways that make her invisible.

This is not because people are cruel. It's because systems—families, workplaces, relationships—adapt to what works. And the strong woman works.

So the load redistributes itself around her.

She is the one who can handle it.

The one who will figure it out.

The one who won't fall apart.

And slowly, strength stops being something she chooses and becomes something she is assigned.

Scripture cautions against this quiet exchange.

"Each one should test their own actions. Then they can take pride in themselves alone, without comparing themselves to someone else, for each one should carry their own load."

—Galatians 6:4–5

There is a difference between helping one another and carrying what was never meant to be yours. But when strength is assumed, that line blurs.

35

Marketable

The strong woman doesn't notice it at first. She keeps showing up the way she always has. She keeps giving because she believes in what she's building—family, work, community, faith. She tells herself this is what responsibility looks like.

But responsibility without reciprocity becomes burden.

And burden, over time, begins to erode joy.

What makes this especially difficult is that the strong woman is often affirmed for the very thing that's costing her. She's told she's capable. Resilient. Impressive. Dependable.

Rarely is she asked if she's tired.

Rarely is she offered relief.

Because the world doesn't worry about the woman who always manages.

This chapter is not about blame.

It's about awareness.

About noticing when strength has quietly crossed the line into expectation—and how difficult it is to step out of a role you never formally accepted, but everyone has grown comfortable with.

For many women, this is the moment clarity begins to sharpen. Not because something dramatic happens, but because a question finally surfaces:

When did my strength stop being a gift and start being a requirement?

I have always been a Type A, overachiever.

Not in a loud way—but in a determined one. When I set my mind to something, I found a way to make it happen. I learned early how to position myself well—how to meet the right people, be in the right rooms, say yes to opportunities that moved me forward.

I applied to college early. I pursued competitive internships. I didn't wait to be invited—I figured out how to qualify. I followed plans. I met milestones. I built a life that, from the outside, looked intentional and well-executed.

Married.

Children.

Career.

All by the age I thought I was supposed to be.

None of this came from pressure alone. Much of it came from confidence—the belief that effort mattered, that preparation paid off, that discipline created options. And that if you never ask for what you want, the answer is almost always, No. And what's the worse thing that can happen?—No. I wasn't reckless. I wasn't drifting. I was purposeful.

And purpose, when it works, gets reinforced.

Success teaches you that forward motion is rewarded. Achievement builds momentum. People trust the person who delivers. Systems rely on the person who doesn't miss.

So I became that person.

The one who figured it out.

The one who followed through.

The one who didn't need much supervision.

At first, this felt empowering.

But strength formed early has a shadow side.

When you prove—again and again—that you can handle things, people stop checking whether you should. When you demonstrate competence consistently, support quietly shifts elsewhere. And when you hit milestones on schedule, the cost of maintaining them is rarely examined.

You don't notice the transition when it happens.

You just notice that you are always the one adjusting. Always the one anticipating. Always the one absorbing pressure so everything else stays on track.

This is how strength becomes expectation.

Not because anyone explicitly demands it—but because the system adapts around your capacity. And once that happens, stepping back feels like failure rather than recalibration.

For women like me, ambition didn't create the problem. Capability did.

Because once you are known as someone who can make things happen, the world assumes you always will.

Even when it costs you.

I learned this pattern long before adulthood.

In middle school, I spent night after night in the arena with my horse, Lightning, practicing for the hunter–jumper circuit in Wellington, Florida. We ran the routines again and again, refining every movement, every transition. I wouldn't leave until we were ready. Ready enough. Polished enough. Controlled enough. One more time.

I loved the discipline. I loved the focus. I loved the feeling of earning confidence through repetition.

But there was a tradeoff I didn't recognize at the time.

Marketable

I took myself too seriously. I wouldn't play pool or relax into the moment until I had practiced on my own and decided I was ready to perform in front of others. Fun came after readiness. Joy came after effort. Presence was postponed until performance felt secure.

At the time, I called this work ethic.

I was proud of my perfectionism. It felt like integrity. Like commitment. Like maturity beyond my years. I believed being "ready" was what kept me safe—from embarrassment, from failure, from disappointment.

And for a while, it worked. I didn't realize what I was missing.

But perfectionism doesn't just sharpen skill. It narrows experience.

Looking back, I can see how much joy it quietly held at arm's length. How many moments passed by while I was preparing for something else. How often I delayed being fully present because I was busy making sure everything was right.

That mindset followed me.

Into leadership.

Into marriage.

Into motherhood.

Into work.

Perfectionism became a filter through which I evaluated myself and the world. It trained me to believe that rest had to be justified, that enjoyment had to be earned, and that readiness was a prerequisite for belonging.

But life doesn't wait for readiness.

And joy doesn't arrive once everything is perfected.

The same discipline that once helped me succeed eventually became the standard I was expected to maintain—by others, and by myself. Strength, control, and preparation stopped being tools and started becoming rules.

Rules that didn't leave much room for spontaneity.

Or softness.

Or simply being in the moment.

Recognizing this didn't mean rejecting excellence. It meant questioning the cost of always striving for it. It meant asking whether being prepared had quietly replaced being present.

And whether the strength I was so proud of had slowly turned into something that was expected—without regard for what it was costing me.

Academically, the pattern held.

I was a straight-A student. Near the top of my class. I thrived on being a top performer—not because I needed praise, but because excellence felt stabilizing. Achievement created order. Results made effort feel worthwhile.

Doing well didn't feel like pressure. It felt like alignment.

Teachers trusted me. Expectations rose naturally. I was given responsibility because I handled it. I was counted on because I delivered. Success reinforced the belief that my role was to perform well—and consistently.

And again, it worked.

But success has a way of quietly raising the bar without asking permission.

When you're a top performer, there's rarely a conversation about capacity. There's no pause to ask whether the pace is sustainable. The assumption is simple: if you've done it before, you can do it again. And again. And again.

So excellence stops being exceptional and becomes expected.

You don't hear thank you as often as you hear of course.

You don't receive support—you receive more responsibility.

You don't get rest—you get the next assignment.

And because you've built your identity around reliability, slowing down feels like letting people down or worse, punishment as you return from a break, and no one can or has stepped in to keep momentum while you rest, but rather, now you have more to do to make up for the time you rested. Opting out feels like regression. Choosing ease feels undeserved.

This is how achievement quietly turns into obligation.

Not through force—but through familiarity.

By the time adulthood arrives, the strong woman doesn't question why she's always the one pushing, carrying, managing. It feels normal. It feels earned. It feels like who she is.

But normal doesn't always mean healthy.

And what once felt like confidence can, over time, begin to feel heavy.

Because being a top performer is energizing—until performance becomes the measure of worth. Until rest feels irresponsible. Until presence feels secondary to productivity.

And that's when strength, once again, becomes expectation.

I didn't avoid asking for help because I didn't believe in community.

I avoided it because experience taught me it rarely worked.

Marketable

When I asked, one of two things usually happened. Either the help wasn't available when I actually needed it—and the responsibility landed back on me anyway, now layered with discouragement, embarrassment, and frustration. Or the help came, but not in a way that met the standard I had already learned to carry.

It fell short of what I knew was required.

So I stopped asking.

Not out of pride—but out of efficiency. It didn't serve me to hand something off only to pick it back up again. It felt easier to stay busy, to perform well, to handle things on my own. At least then I knew where everything stood.

Control became my safety net.

I learned how to multitask in motion. I functioned best when everything was moving—when momentum kept the system upright. As long as I stayed engaged, attentive, and active, nothing fell apart.

And I didn't drop balls.

Dropping balls wasn't an option. Not because I was incapable—but because I had seen what happened when things slowed down. Gaps appeared. Expectations were missed. Loose ends surfaced. Slowing down didn't feel like rest—it felt like risk.

So I stayed in motion.

Busyness wasn't chaos. It was containment.

The irony is that this kind of strength looks admirable from the outside. It reads as competence. Reliability. Leadership. But internally, it creates a quiet rigidity. A belief that steadiness must be maintained at all costs, and that pausing will expose weakness rather than restore capacity.

Over time, asking for help stopped feeling like collaboration and started feeling like liability.

And once that happens, strength doesn't just become expectation—it becomes isolation.

The strong woman isn't unsupported because she doesn't deserve help. She's unsupported because she learned, early and repeatedly, that depending on others came with consequences she couldn't afford.

So she learned to carry more.

And carry it well.

Staying in motion made me feel important.
Invincible.

Strong.

Useful.

Unstoppable.

As long as everything was moving, I felt essential to the system. My effort mattered. My presence had weight. I could point to results and say, This is why I do what I do.

Until I stopped.

Not abruptly. Not dramatically. But intentionally.

The system I had built—the one fueled by momentum, multitasking, and constant output—stopped working the moment I asked it to slow down. And in that pause, I began setting boundaries where there had never been any before.

At first, the boundaries were practical. Monitoring of emails but not responding unless an expressed emergency. If it wasn't a requirement, was it necessary for my job? If it wasn't, I weighed whether it added or took away my peace. I evaluated personal boundaries, where I once performed over and beyond with usage of words like "family" in the workplace, but once I removed the weight from what was expected and what was inferred, the boundaries became non-negotiable. Fewer obligations. Clearer limits. More protected time.

What they gave me was unexpected.

They gave me time with my family—, real time, not background presence. Time with friends without rushing. Time to sit quietly without immediately filling the space.

They gave me pause.

And in that pause, I revisited a question I hadn't examined in years: Why am I doing all of this?

Not the surface answer. The deeper one.

Who was I doing it for?

What was it costing me?

Was this pace still serving the life I wanted—or only the life I had learned to sustain?

The answers weren't immediate. But they were honest.

Time revealed things I had been too busy to see. How fast my children had grown. How much of my own life had passed in motion. How close I was to a milestone I had once assumed would mean nothing at all.

Turning forty surprised me.

Marketable

I thought it would be just another year. Another marker on a calendar. Something I would pass through without much reflection.

It wasn't.

It became a quiet reckoning—not with regret, but with reality. With how quickly time moves. With how finite energy is. With how much of my strength had been poured outward without asking whether it was still aligned.

That realization didn't dismantle my life.

It clarified it. And the choices I made because of that clarity, may have arguably, been the most important ones for my future.

Strength, I learned, doesn't disappear when you stop proving it. It changes shape. It becomes discernment instead of endurance. Presence instead of pressure. Intention instead of inertia.

And expectation—once examined—loses its grip.

Because what I finally understood is this:

Being strong is not the same as being essential to everything.

Being useful is not the same as being fulfilled.

And being unstoppable is not the same as being alive.

This chapter is not about rejecting strength.

It's about reclaiming it.

On your terms.

In this season.

With eyes open to what matters now.

You are never starting from zero again.

Hold This

Your competence is a gift, not a contract. Just because you can handle it does not mean you were assigned to carry it.

Try This

- Where did my 'I can do it' turn into 'I must do it'?
- Who benefits from my overfunctioning - and what would change if I paused?
- What is the simplest sentence I can use to communicate a boundary?

Practice: Draft one boundary line: 'I can do X by Y.' or 'I'm not available for X, but I can help with Y.'

Chapter 4
When the Strong Woman Steps Back

"Silence is heavy when your story has a signature on it."
— Brittany P. Webb

When a strong woman steps back, the world doesn't fall apart.

But it does notice.

Systems shift. Rhythms change. Expectations surface—sometimes quietly, sometimes uncomfortably. The absence of her constant motion creates a pause that reveals how much she was holding together without acknowledgment.

This is where many women feel disoriented.

Not because they've done something wrong—but because they've disrupted a pattern others had come to rely on. When strength has been consistent for a long time, its absence—even temporary—feels like instability to those who benefited from it.

This isn't usually malicious.

It's structural.

Families adapt to the person who anticipates. Workplaces adjust around the one who delivers. Relationships lean into the person who smooths things over. And when that person steps back—even slightly—gaps appear.

What used to be invisible becomes visible.

Tasks go undone. Emotions surface. Decisions linger. The system hesitates, waiting for the familiar force that once kept everything moving.

This is often when doubt creeps in.

Maybe I shouldn't have pulled back.

Maybe I misjudged this.

Maybe it really does all fall on me.

But that moment of hesitation is not evidence that the boundary was wrong.

It's evidence that the system was built around your overfunctioning.

The strong woman stepping back doesn't create dysfunction. It reveals where balance was already missing.

This is the part few people talk about: when you stop compensating, others are given the opportunity to step forward—or to recognize what they've taken for granted. Sometimes they do. Sometimes they don't. But either way, clarity replaces assumption.

And clarity is uncomfortable at first.

Because it removes the illusion that everything was working effortlessly. It shows where effort was being absorbed by one person, quietly and consistently.

This chapter is not about blame or resentment.

It's about recalibration.

About learning to tolerate the discomfort of change without rushing in to fix it. About allowing others the dignity of responsibility. About resisting the urge to resume old roles simply because silence or inefficiency feels unfamiliar.

When the strong woman steps back, she isn't abandoning the life she built.

She's making room for it to become more honest.

The first change was subtle—but decisive.

I stopped dropping everything and jumping at the level people expected.

Not because I didn't care. Not because I was disengaged. But because immediacy had quietly become an expectation I never agreed to. I began offering realistic timeframes—for responses, for decisions, for deliverables—and I honored them.

Urgency stopped being assumed.

So did availability.

Another shift followed closely behind it: I stopped allowing full access to my friendship, my time, and stopped apologizing for things I hadn't actually done wrong.

This was harder than I expected.

I noticed how often sorry came out of my mouth automatically—before I even observed indicators that it was necessary. Before there was confirmation that harm had occurred. Before context had fully formed.

Apologies had become a reflex. A way to keep the peace. A way to soften edges. A way to protect myself in case something I said or did was perceived differently than I intended.

I wasn't apologizing for wrongdoing.

I was apologizing preemptively—for existence, for boundaries, for taking up space.

So I started a quiet transition I half-jokingly called Sorry, Not Sorry, like the Demi Lovato anthem, playing in the background as I muttered the words out loud.

I paid attention to the moments when sorry wanted to surface—and asked myself a better question: Am I actually sorry? Did I act without integrity? Did I cause harm I needed to repair? Or was I simply uncomfortable letting others sit with their own reactions?

Most of the time, it was the latter.

Letting people figure things out on their own was uncomfortable. Letting someone else step in—especially if they didn't do it the way I would have—was even harder. I had been trained to equate stepping in with being responsible, and stepping back with being careless.

But something surprising happened.

Things still got done.

Maybe not exactly how I would have done them. Maybe not as quickly. Maybe not as polished. But they got done. And the world didn't wobble the way I had feared.

What did shift was my internal landscape.

I had more peace.

More margin.

More space to breathe and be present.

And I lost the need to care as much about the way things were done. They were done. And people were satisfied with the outcome, even when it wasn't what I would have done. It was okay. And I gained space and peace along the way.

Once I saw that sharing responsibility didn't lead to chaos—but to balance—I began to trust the process. Accountability no longer rested solely on my shoulders. Ownership became distributed. Expectations adjusted.

Stepping back didn't diminish my contribution.

It refined it.

I was still dependable—but not depleted. Still engaged—but not overextended. Still caring—but no longer carrying what wasn't mine to hold.

This is the quiet work of recalibration. It doesn't announce itself. It doesn't come with applause. But it changes everything—because it allows strength to coexist with sustainability.

And that kind of strength lasts.

Just because I could do it all didn't mean I had to be the one who did.

Marketable

That distinction changed everything.

For so long, capability had quietly turned into obligation. If I could handle something, I assumed it was mine. If I didn't step in, I feared things would stall, fall apart, or reflect poorly on me. Responsibility followed ability without question.

But when I stopped volunteering for everything and being "voluntold", and the automatic answer, something unexpected happened.

Space opened.

When I wasn't the one doing everything, someone else had the opportunity to step in—and step up. That was true at home and at work. Teaching my children how to do laundry, fold clothes, vacuum, mow the yard. Delegating more intentionally in professional settings.

At first, it was uncomfortable.

There were moments when things took longer. When outcomes weren't exactly how I would have done them. When timelines stretched or results looked different than what I was used to producing. There were real risks—time, money, momentum, reputation.

And yes, sometimes it felt like it might set us back.

But every time I resisted the urge to take it back over, something shifted.

I moved one step closer to not being the only one responsible for everything getting done.

There was another truth I had to face.

My expectations—often unspoken—were high. Not because I demanded perfection from others, although I often hoped they would perform at the level that I did—in my head, it would make *my* life easier, but because I had trained myself to deliver it consistently. Over time, that standard became intimidating.

When people believe they can't meet the bar, they stop trying. When the risk of falling short feels greater than the benefit of stepping in, they step back. And without realizing it, I had created a system where it felt safer for me to do everything than for someone else to attempt it.

That wasn't anyone's failure. It was a pattern I hadn't known how to interrupt—until I stepped back far enough to see it.

It was a communication gap.

By loosening my grip—not just on outcomes, but on expectations—I made space for participation. I learned to make room for learning, growth, and effort, not just execution. And in doing so, I stopped being the only one capable of carrying the load.

Over time, I noticed another change in myself. I stopped nitpicking. I loosened my grip on how things had to look. I began to recognize that there was more than one way to reach a good outcome—and that "perfect" wasn't always necessary to move forward.

What others produced wasn't wrong.

It was different.

And often, it was more than sufficient.

Letting go of control didn't lower the standard—it widened the process. It allowed collaboration to replace isolation. Growth to replace dependency. And peace to replace constant vigilance.

I was still invested. Still engaged. Still responsible.

I just wasn't carrying it alone anymore.

And the surprise was this: the world didn't become less functional. It became more balanced. I gained time. I gained presence. I gained joy. I could complete something and actually move on—without replaying it, fixing it, or managing the aftermath.

Stepping back didn't diminish my strength.

It redistributed it.

And in that redistribution, I found something I hadn't realized I was missing—freedom to live without controlling every outcome, and the ability to be happy with what was good, instead of exhausted by chasing what I believed had to be perfect.

You are never starting from zero again.

Hold This

Stepping back doesn't make you less loving. It makes room for shared strength, shared responsibility, and healthier rhythm.

Try This

- Where do I rescue before anyone has a chance to try?
- What emotion shows up when I don't fix it - guilt, fear, irritation, anxiety?
- What would it look like to stay present without taking over?

Practice: Choose one task you normally 'save.' Let someone else attempt it. Stay calm. Let it be imperfect.

Chapter 5
Responsibility Is Not the Same as Self-Sacrifice

"Some pivots happen in public. Mine happened in the quiet."
— Brittany P. Webb

For a long time, I believed responsibility meant availability.

If something needed attention, I gave it mine.

If someone needed help, I adjusted.

If there was a gap, I filled it.

Responsibility, to me, looked like showing up first and leaving last. It meant anticipating needs before they were spoken. It meant staying alert so nothing slipped through the cracks.

And I was good at it.

But somewhere along the way, responsibility stopped being a value and became a measure of worth. The more I carried, the more legitimate I felt. The more indispensable I became, the more secure I believed I was.

That's a dangerous equation.

Because responsibility, when untethered from self-awareness, quietly demands self-sacrifice. And self-sacrifice, when it becomes a pattern rather than a choice, erodes identity.

I didn't realize how often I had confused being responsible with being necessary. How easily I equated stepping back with letting people down. How deeply I believed that if I wasn't actively contributing, I was failing in some way.

This belief didn't come from one place. It was reinforced everywhere—at work, at home, in leadership, in faith. Responsibility was praised. Availability was rewarded. Self-denial was spiritualized.

But nowhere did anyone pause to ask: At what cost?

The truth is, responsibility was never meant to require self-erasure.

There is a difference between being dependable and being depleted. Between showing up and disappearing inside what you're carrying. Between serving others and abandoning yourself.

I had crossed that line without realizing it.

When I began setting boundaries, slowing my response time, and allowing others to take ownership, I wasn't becoming less responsible. I was becoming more intentional. I was choosing how and where my energy belonged instead of letting it be claimed automatically.

That distinction changed my internal dialogue.

Instead of asking, Who needs me right now?

I began asking, What is actually mine to hold?

Instead of reacting to urgency, I learned to respond to alignment.

Responsibility stopped being about constant output and started becoming about stewardship—of my time, my energy, my relationships, and my health. I could still care deeply without carrying everything personally. I could still contribute meaningfully without being consumed by the process.

And perhaps most importantly, I learned that stepping back didn't make me less valuable.

It made me more whole.

This chapter is about untangling that lie—the one that tells capable women they must always be available to be worthy. It's about learning that responsibility can coexist with rest, and that faithfulness does not require exhaustion.

Because responsibility, rightly understood, does not ask you to disappear.

It asks you to be present.

Responsibility Is Not the Same as Self-Sacrifice

I believed I was more valuable if I was always available.

More useful if I was the most helpful.

More necessary if I was ready—on standby—for whatever reaction the moment required.

Availability felt like worth.

As a mom of three, life trained me well for this. There were always surprises. A child wakes up sick. Broken Bone. Emergency Appendectomy. Someone's projectile vomiting and didn't make it to the toilet, and your carpet is still 1980's shag carpet—Yeah, that one was a fun night! "Hey mom, I have a project due tomorrow that requires supplies, a poster board, a typed-up paper with sources and printed out pictures, oh, and—a costume. And can you be there? It starts at 8:15". You know how it goes. On your toes, fire drills, pop-quizzes. Life as we know it.

And as work would have it, managing a team sometimes is no different. When grown adults entertain similar patterns, appearing to need life-management skills, calling out for "tummy" aches, late nights, last-minute alarm issues, unexcused absences, and what appears to be any excuse to not have to be held accountable. Sound the alarm, here we go again. Gaps need filling. And with timelines and deadlines and deliverables, you learn to live on the edge of readiness, reprioritization, and execution.

So I did.

I carried the purse with all the aids. The sprays and solvents under the counter for quick cleanups. The metaphorical pocket fire extinguisher for the next fire, at work and at home. A full toolkit of solutions, just in case.

I thought this was responsibility.

But over time, it became something else.

I wasn't just responding to problems—I was anticipating them. Expecting them. Bracing for them. My nervous system stayed primed for interruption, trained to believe that something was always about to go wrong.

And when you live like that long enough, you start to see problems everywhere.

Not because they're actually happening more often—but because you've conditioned yourself to thrive on being needed. On being the fixer. On being the one who steps in before anyone else has to.

That realization was uncomfortable. And exhausting.

Because when I stopped expecting everything to fall apart, I noticed something surprising: it rarely did. And when challenges did arise, they were often smaller than I had imagined. Manageable. Momentary. Not the emergencies I had rehearsed for.

The chaos I thought I was preventing had largely been projected.

When I became more present—and less perpetually available— something shifted externally as well. People respected the time I gave them because it was no longer unlimited. My attention carried weight because it wasn't constantly on offer.

I wasn't withdrawing.

I was valuing myself.

And that value recalibrated everything.

People don't learn to respect your time because you ask them to. They learn because you do. When you prioritize your life intentionally, others adjust to the signal you send.

For me, that priority became clear:
God.
Family.
Friends.
Work.

Play.

Other.

Not reacting to life as it rushed toward me without order or discernment—but choosing what I would respond to, what I would hold, and what I would let pass.

Responsibility, I learned, doesn't require constant readiness. It requires wisdom. Presence. Discernment. The ability to trust that not everything is urgent—and not everything is yours.

When you stop performing availability and start honoring alignment, responsibility becomes lighter. More honest. More sustainable.

And you discover something essential:

You were never meant to live on standby.

What was hardest to stop responding to wasn't crisis.

It was noise.

All the things that didn't really matter—but once had constant access to my attention. Opinions. Minor urgencies. Background chatter. Conversations that didn't require resolution. Decisions that didn't need to be made today—or at all.

For a long time, I treated noise like obligation.

If something entered my awareness, I assumed it deserved a response. If it lingered, I felt compelled to resolve it. Silence felt negligent. Delay felt risky.

But noise has a way of masquerading as importance.

When I slowed down enough to notice, I realized how much energy I had been spending on things that neither shaped my values nor moved my life forward. They simply filled space. And I had been letting them.

So I made a different choice.

I let things wait.

I stopped answering immediately. I stopped reacting reflexively. I stopped deciding just to quiet the discomfort of indecision. I allowed unfinished conversations to remain unfinished. I allowed questions to sit unanswered. I allowed silence to exist without rushing to fill it.

And nothing broke.

In fact, something steadied.

The absence of constant reaction created room for discernment. I could feel the difference between what was truly mine to respond to and what was merely passing through. What once felt urgent revealed itself as optional. What once felt heavy revealed itself as noise.

Peace didn't arrive because life got quieter.

It arrived because I stopped amplifying what didn't matter.

This is where responsibility becomes wisdom.

Not everything needs your voice.

Not everything needs your decision.

Not everything needs your energy.

Choosing when not to engage is not avoidance. It's stewardship. It's trusting yourself—and God—with timing, clarity, and outcome.

When noise no longer dictates your attention, presence becomes possible again. You hear what matters. You respond with intention. You act from alignment rather than urgency.

And the life you're living begins to feel less crowded.

Not because there's less happening—but because you're no longer giving equal weight to everything that asks for you.

For a long time, I believed I could influence outcomes.

And sometimes, that's true.

There are moments when effort matters. When preparation, conversation, and action shape what comes next. There are spaces where my voice is meant to be present and my decisions carry weight.

But I've learned that not every situation belongs to me.

Some outcomes are already in motion—set into place by something far bigger than my effort, my worry, or my control. And when I step into those spaces, trying to manage what was never mine to orchestrate, I lose my footing.

I step into territory where God is big.

And good.

And already at work.

That's where I had been spending far too much time.

Trying to influence what didn't require my intervention. Trying to prepare for futures that hadn't arrived. Trying to preempt pain, disappointment, or uncertainty by rehearsing it early.

The cost of that was subtle but real.

It pulled me out of center.

Out of presence.

Out of peace.

Worry crept in—not because something had gone wrong, but because I had wandered too far ahead of the moment I was actually living. I tipped into unrest by attempting to solve what wasn't yet mine to face.

That kind of anticipation doesn't protect us.

It drains us.

I realized that staying grounded required discernment—not about whether something might happen, but about where I was meant to stand right now. I didn't need to borrow trouble from a future that hadn't arrived. I didn't need to live inside outcomes I couldn't confirm.

What I needed was to return—to the present, to truth, to peace.

Even when the future held unknowns.

Even when answers weren't immediate.

Even when outcomes felt unsettled.

Peace, I learned, doesn't come from certainty.

It comes from trust.

Trust that I don't need to start suffering now for something that may never happen. Trust that God is already holding what I'm tempted to manage. Trust that my role is not to control the future, but to remain faithful in the moment I've been given.

When I stopped trying to influence what wasn't mine, I felt steadier. More aligned. Less reactive. I could respond when it was time—without staying perpetually braced for impact.

Responsibility doesn't mean standing watch over every possible outcome.

Sometimes, it means knowing when to step back and let God do what only He can.

And when I stayed there—anchored in the present, grounded in truth, attentive to peace—I found that whatever came next could be met with clarity instead of fear.

That's not passivity.

That's wisdom.

You are never starting from zero again.

Hold This

Responsibility without self-care becomes self-sacrifice. Love is not measured by depletion.

Try This

Marketable

- Where do I give past my capacity and then feel resentful?
- What do I keep doing because I don't want to disappoint anyone?
- If I treated myself like a neighbor, what would I stop demanding of me?

Practice: Write one sentence: 'I can be loving and still say no.' Repeat it when guilt shows up.

Chapter 6
Peace Did Arrive, But Not All at Once

"Peace doesn't flood in; it seeps in."
— Brittany P. Webb

But it did not arrive alone.

When I left that job, I felt two things at once—relief and panic, certainty and fear, grounding and free fall. The decision itself was settled in my spirit, but my nervous system hadn't caught up yet.

I knew God was with me.

I knew I had made the right choice.

And I still spiraled.

Bound by Silence

I can't share every detail of what happened next. Not because I'm hiding the truth—because I'm honoring it. There were documents signed, terms to respect, and lines I chose not to cross. But I can tell you what it felt like.

I walked away with my head high and my character intact. And I walked away with a kind of silence around me—an agreement that limited what I could say and where I could go next. A season that demanded integrity when my emotions wanted to defend myself.

That's when the fear got practical. It wasn't only grief or shock—it was the question of: What happens when you can't simply pivot? When you can't freely explain the story, and you can't freely pursue the next opportunity?

Looking back, I know I had been deeply relied on. My responsibilities didn't disappear when I left—they redistributed. More than one person had to absorb what I had carried. That should have felt validating. Instead, it exposed something I needed to face: I had been measuring worth by how hard I would be to "replace", knowing that I was replaceable, but also certain that there wasn't anyone quite like me out there. Psalm 139:14 says, " I praise you because I am fearfully and wonderfully made; your works are wonderful, I know that full well."

So the work I now had before me became different. Not proving I mattered. Re-learning that my value was never owned by a job title, a culture, or a company's request for compliance that I chose to deny. Deny access to me. Deny a request that would compromise of character and integrity, that would severe my care for the situation and the people involved. Their choice did not get to be my definition.

This was the moment I stopped waiting for external confirmation—and started recovering the asset underneath everything: my clarity, my steadiness, my faith, and my ability to create a life that still fit me. This was an external circumstance. Internally, I needed to draw the line.

That tension—peace existing alongside panic—was disorienting. Not because I doubted the decision, but because the silence afterward was deafening. The structure was gone. The noise stopped. And suddenly there was nothing buffering the questions.

Peace was present.

But not speaking louder than fear was.

In the days and weeks that followed, emotions came in waves. Relief would surface, then grief. Gratitude would give way to anxiety. Hope would rise, followed closely by uncertainty. Sometimes all of it in the same hour.

But underneath the emotional churn, something remained steady.

Not calm.

Not clarity.

But knowing.

The kind of knowing that doesn't argue with your feelings, but outlasts them.

Peace, I learned, isn't the absence of panic. It's the presence of trust while panic passes through. It doesn't silence fear—it anchors you beneath it. The feelings were real. The uncertainty was real. The financial pressure was real.

The decision was no longer up for debate.

That distinction mattered.

Because when emotions surged, they no longer got to vote. They could speak—but they didn't get to steer. I didn't feel peaceful all the time. I didn't feel brave most days. But I no longer felt torn.

God was with me.

I had listened.

I had acted in integrity.

Everything else could be worked through.

After the initial rush of emotion began to settle, peace started showing up in quieter ways.

Not as certainty—but as steadiness.

I noticed it first in my body. I wasn't bracing as much. My jaw unclenched. My shoulders dropped. I slept without waking up rehearsing conversations or calculating outcomes. My breath slowed—not because everything was resolved, but because I no longer felt responsible for resolving everything at once.

Peace didn't mean I stopped thinking.

It meant my thoughts no longer spiraled unchecked.

When worry surfaced, it didn't automatically pull me forward into imagined futures. I learned how to bring myself back—to what was true right now. To what I knew. To what I could actually tend to in the present moment.

Scripture speaks to this kind of peace gently and often:

"Do not worry about tomorrow, for tomorrow will worry about itself. Each day has enough trouble of its own."

—Matthew 6:34

For years, I had lived as though tomorrow's trouble needed my attention today. Peace arrived when I finally believed it didn't.

Another shift followed: my relationship with silence changed.

Silence no longer felt like something was wrong. It stopped signaling danger or abandonment. It became space—space to notice, to listen, to discern. I didn't rush to fill it with noise, explanation, or action.

In that quiet, I could hear myself again.

Peace also changed how I made decisions.

I stopped forcing clarity. I stopped pressuring myself to know what came next. Instead of asking, What should I do? I began asking, What feels aligned right now? And if the answer wasn't clear, I waited.

Waiting used to feel irresponsible.

Now, it felt wise.

"In quietness and trust is your strength."

—Isaiah 30:15

Trust became the anchor. Not trust that everything would work out perfectly—but trust that I didn't need to outrun uncertainty to be okay.

Peace didn't remove hard days. There were still moments of grief for what was familiar, fear about finances, and discomfort in not having a clear roadmap. But peace meant those feelings no longer defined the day.

They came and went.

I stayed.

Marketable

What surprised me most was how peace affected my energy. I had more of it—not because life demanded less, but because I stopped wasting it on things that didn't require my involvement. I no longer spent hours replaying conversations, second-guessing decisions, or managing perceptions.

Peace conserved energy.

And with that energy came presence.

I was more available to the people in front of me—without being available to everything. I could enjoy moments without scanning for what might go wrong next. I could feel joy without immediately wondering how long it would last.

Peace wasn't fragile anymore.

It was practiced.

Over time, I learned that peace isn't something you arrive at and keep forever. It's something you return to—again and again—by choosing presence over prediction, trust over control, and truth over fear.

That choice doesn't eliminate uncertainty.

It teaches you how to live well inside it.

Peace also began to show up in how my days were shaped.

I stopped crowding them.

I no longer stacked commitments back-to-back simply because I could. I built margin where there had once been efficiency. Space between meetings. Space between conversations. Space between expectations.

At first, that space felt indulgent.

Then it felt necessary.

I learned that peace requires room to breathe. When every moment is spoken for, there is no place for reflection to land. No place for intuition to surface. No place for God to speak quietly instead of urgently.

My mornings changed. I wasn't rushing to prove productivity before the day began. I allowed the day to meet me where I was instead of sprinting toward it already depleted. I let stillness be part of the rhythm rather than a reward for finishing everything else.

Peace also reshaped my relationships.

I listened more and explained less. I answered questions without overjustifying. I allowed others to have reactions without rushing to soothe them. I didn't confuse someone else's discomfort with my responsibility.

This was uncomfortable at first.

When you stop managing emotional outcomes, relationships recalibrate. Some people lean in. Some pull away. Some don't know what to do with the quieter version of you who no longer fills every gap.

But peace made space for honesty.

I could be present without performing reassurance. I could love without absorbing anxiety. I could support without carrying what wasn't mine. And in that shift, relationships became more mutual—less dependent on my regulation and more rooted in shared responsibility.

Peace did not make me passive.

It made me discerning.

I began to recognize peace as a signal—not avoidance, not apathy, but alignment. If something consistently disrupted my peace, I paid attention. Not everything that causes discomfort should be avoided, but not everything that demands energy deserves it either.

I stopped forcing decisions simply to quiet my mind. I stopped chasing clarity out of fear. I allowed answers to unfold instead of extracting them prematurely.

Scripture reminds us:

"The peace of God, which transcends all understanding, will guard your hearts and your minds."

—Philippians 4:7

Guarding is active. It's protective. It suggests boundaries—not openness to everything, but protection over what matters most.

Peace became my filter.
Not Is this urgent?
But Is this aligned?
Not *can* I handle this?
But Is this mine to handle right now?
This didn't simplify life.
It clarified it.

Some days were still hard. Some decisions still carried weight. Some unknowns remained unresolved. But peace allowed me to move through them without losing my center. Without bracing for impact. Without assuming the worst before it arrived.

Peace also softened my self-talk.

Marketable

I stopped narrating my worth through productivity. I stopped measuring the day by what I accomplished. I began to recognize presence as enough. Faithfulness as sufficient. Rest as legitimate.

And slowly, I trusted myself again.

Not because I had all the answers—but because I knew how to return to peace when I lost it.

That's the kind of peace that lasts.

Not the absence of challenge.

Not the guarantee of ease.

But the steady confidence that you are not required to manage everything to live well.

Peace, I learned, is not a destination.

It is a practice.

And once it becomes familiar, you stop chasing it—and start living from it.

You are never starting from zero again.

Hold This

Silence can be strategy. It can be protection. It can be holy restraint - without becoming self-erasure.

Try This

- What is one truth I can speak without naming names?
- What am I allowed to say - safely - about what this season is doing in me?
- What is the difference between silence that protects me and silence that shrinks me?

Practice: Write one paragraph titled 'What I can say.' Keep it entirely about you (your body, your faith, your clarity, your grief, your growth). No company details. Just you.

Chapter 7
Living From Alignment Instead of Approval

"Approval is loud. Alignment is steady."
— Brittany P. Webb

Peace didn't arrive all at once—but once it started to arrive, it made room for something I hadn't trusted in a long time: my own compass. That's where alignment began.

For a long time, I didn't trust myself.

That may sound surprising, considering how capable I appeared. I made decisions. I carried responsibility. I handled complexity. But underneath all of that was constant monitoring.

I double-checked my instincts. I replayed conversations. I second-guessed decisions long after they were made—not because I lacked wisdom, but because I had learned to outsource trust: to systems, to expectations, to approval, to other people's reactions.

Overfunctioning doesn't just exhaust you—it erodes your confidence in your own inner compass. Letting go of constant management created space… and it also exposed how unfamiliar self-trust had become. At first, the quiet felt disorienting.

Trust didn't return instantly. It rebuilt slowly—in small moments where I followed an instinct and didn't explain it, where I made a decision and didn't over-justify it, where I let the outcome be what it was and stayed intact anyway.

And once that took hold, I could finally see something I'd missed for years: approval doesn't always look like people-pleasing. Sometimes it looks like over-explaining. Sometimes it looks like staying agreeable. Sometimes it looks like shaping yourself just enough to avoid resistance.

For most of my life, I didn't think I was living for approval.

I wasn't chasing praise. I wasn't seeking validation in obvious ways. I was capable, confident, accomplished. I made decisions and followed through on them.

I didn't need applause—but I did want to be understood. I wanted things to go smoothly. I wanted to minimize disruption, tension, and disappointment. And without realizing it, I often adjusted myself to make that happen.

Approval lived in the margins.

It showed up in how carefully I framed decisions. How much context I gave before saying no. How often I justified choices that were already aligned. I wasn't asking permission outright—but I was still negotiating.

Integrity changed that.

As my self-trust stabilized, I stopped seeking confirmation outside myself before moving forward. I didn't need everyone to agree. I didn't need every decision to land comfortably. I began choosing what fit—even when it wasn't immediately understood.

This didn't make me rigid.

It made me clear.

Living from integrity meant my yes and no carried the same tone. Calm. Unhurried. Unapologetic. I wasn't pushing against people—I was standing in myself.

That shift changed how relationships functioned.

Some people adjusted easily. Others struggled with the quieter, firmer version of me who no longer filled gaps or softened edges automatically. I didn't rush to manage their reactions. I trusted them to find their footing just as I was finding mine.

Alignment doesn't eliminate friction.

It removes confusion.

In work, this looked like choosing projects that matched my values instead of just my abilities. It meant letting go of opportunities that would have required me to perform a version of myself I no longer inhabited. I stopped equating opportunity with obligation.

Not everything that I could do was something I should do.

Alignment simplified decisions.

Instead of asking, Will this be well-received?

I asked, Is this true to who I am now?

Instead of asking, Does this make sense to others?

I asked, Does this make sense to me?

That internal clarity reduced the need for explanation. When decisions are aligned, they don't require convincing. They may invite questions—but they don't need defense.

Living from integrity also changed how I handled disagreement.

I no longer felt compelled to persuade. I could state my position and allow others to hold theirs. I didn't need resolution to feel secure. I didn't need consensus to feel grounded.

Approval had once functioned as a safety net.

Alignment became my anchor.

The difference was subtle but powerful. One required constant calibration. The other required honesty. One kept me scanning the room. Doing what I had grown to do so well, sensing other's comfortability levels and unspoken reactions. Tempted to fix the tension. But the other, it kept me rooted and secure, regardless of others experiences.

When you live from integrity, you stop editing yourself in anticipation of reaction. You trust that what's meant to connect will—and what doesn't, won't. And either outcome is okay.

This isn't about becoming indifferent.

It's about becoming whole.

Integrity doesn't ask you to be louder or smaller. It asks you to be accurate. To live in congruence with your values, your faith, and your capacity. And own it.

And once you do, something settles.

You stop asking, Is this okay?

And start living as if it already is.

Leaving the known and stepping into the unknown tested alignment in ways comfort never could.

After I left my job, I expected momentum. Instead, I met resistance. Finding a traditional role proved more difficult than I anticipated. Doors didn't open quickly. Structure fell away. And without immediate opportunities to overwork or perform, I was left with space.

Time to heal.

Time to be present with my family.

Time to sit with uncertainty instead of outrunning it.

Eventually, I moved again.

In The Uncommon AffAIr, I wrote about the creation of Beacon Creative—a partnership that gave me structure when I needed motion. It was a way back into building. A way to re-engage creativity, momentum, and purpose after a season of stillness.

Beacon Creative mattered. It served its purpose.

Marketable

But even there, something became clear.

I was still operating within someone else's framework. Still calibrating decisions against shared expectations. Still needing alignment from outside myself before fully trusting my direction.

Approval hadn't disappeared.

It had just changed form.

That realization led to a harder decision.

For the first time, I chose to leave security and safety, and step fully on my own.

Not because partnership was wrong—but because alignment required ownership. I couldn't build what I was meant to build while waiting for consensus. I had to answer questions no one else could answer for me:

What do I want to create?

What do I believe in deeply?

What am I no longer willing to do?

Those answers didn't come with guarantees. But they came with clarity.

And this time, clarity was enough.

That was the moment alignment stopped being conceptual and became operational. I wasn't asking permission anymore. In fact, that wasn't even an option. I had to learn research, consult, and make the best-informed decision, and trust it. And eventually learn from it or confirm with it.

And I wasn't performing vision inside someone else's structure, either.

I was building from conviction.

The kind that when you feel like you are building an ark like Noah did, with no clear understanding of why, but you know that your calling isn't to know the why, but find peace in submission, and follow through that comes with obedience.

That choice didn't remove uncertainty.

It gave me direction. And I'll be quite honest, I struggled with not being able to see past the next step that God would reveal to me in His time, but nothing more as I built brick by brick, walking through revealed doors, one by one, only to find another step revealed.

Building on my own required a different kind of courage than I had practiced before.

There was no one to check in with. No shared vision to calibrate against. No consensus to lean on when decisions felt heavy. The absence of approval was both freeing and unsettling.

Alignment asks you to stand alone long enough to hear yourself clearly.

At first, that solitude felt exposed. When you've spent years refining ideas through collaboration, leadership structures, or external validation, making decisions in isolation can feel reckless. I had moments where I wondered if I was being irresponsible—if I was confusing confidence with stubbornness.

But alignment doesn't shout.

It settles.

I learned to sit with ideas longer. To test them against my values instead of against anticipated reactions. To ask not only *Will* this work? but Does this fit who I am now?

That question became my compass.

Living from integrity also required me to grieve certain things quietly. The comfort of shared responsibility. The reassurance of being backed by a system. Shared Accountability. The ease of saying we instead of I.

But grief is often a sign that something mattered—not that it should be reclaimed.

Letting go of approval meant letting go of the version of myself who felt safest when mirrored by others. Not simply executing someone else's ideas or agreed upon plans, but rather proving out an idea of my own and finding the resources, developing a plan, and pulling the trigger to make it happen. I had to trust that my clarity didn't need witnesses to be real.

That trust reshaped my pace.

I stopped rushing to prove traction. I allowed ideas to mature. I built intentionally, even when it looked slower from the outside. I learned that alignment isn't always the most

efficient—but it is sustainable.

Some days were quiet. Too quiet.

Without immediate affirmation, I had to practice believing in the work before results showed up. I had to intentionally quiet the little voice in my head that was constantly asking, "And tell me why again we are doing this?" It didn't take much to move me from pure confidence to complete doubt once I leaned into that little voice, so I had tune it out. Listen to music. Hum while I worked. I learned how to keep moving without applause. How to stay anchored when feedback was absent or delayed.

That was uncomfortable.

But it was also grounding.

Approval trains you to look outward for confirmation. Alignment trains you to listen inward for resonance. And resonance doesn't always come with urgency—it comes with steadiness.

Marketable

Over time, I noticed how alignment simplified my decisions.

I no longer weighed every option equally. Some choices fell away naturally—not because they were bad, but because they didn't belong to this version of me. Opportunities that once would have tempted me now felt neutral. Invitations didn't automatically require a response.

Alignment reduced noise.

It also clarified boundaries.

I didn't need to explain why something wasn't a fit. I didn't need to justify my direction to make it palatable. When something didn't align, the answer was simply no—and that no carried peace instead of defensiveness.

Living from integrity didn't make me less collaborative.

It made me more honest.

I could engage without disappearing. I could partner without shrinking. I could contribute without abandoning myself. And that changed the quality of every interaction.

Alignment also changed how I handled doubt.

Doubt didn't disappear—but it no longer dictated movement. I learned to distinguish between fear and misalignment. Fear is loud and urgent. Misalignment is quiet and persistent.

Listening for the difference mattered.

When fear showed up, I stayed curious. Discerning. Am I supposed to lean in here, grow from this experience, through the fear and discomfort. Or is this truly something I should stay away from? And when true misalignment surfaced, I paid attention. Ears perked, everything else around, silenced, like the posture of a dog when the doorknob starts to turn, trying to read all the signs of whether it's their favorite person or whether they need to be on alert. Alignment doesn't demand certainty—it asks for integrity.

And integrity, I learned, is enough to keep moving.

Living from integrity instead of approval didn't guarantee success.

It guaranteed congruence.

And that congruence made life feel lighter—not easier, but truer. I wasn't performing confidence. I was inhabiting it. I wasn't chasing reassurance. I was standing in conviction.

Approval had once felt like safety.

Alignment became home.

You are never starting from zero again.

Hold This

Alignment often feels like loss before it feels like freedom. When you stop living for approval, the noise gets louder - and then it gets clearer.

Try This

- Where am I choosing peace but calling it selfish?

- What am I doing for approval that I no longer want to maintain?

- What is one aligned choice I can make without explaining it?

Practice: Two columns: 'Approval' vs. 'Alignment.' List three decisions. Choose one small aligned action today.

Chapter 8
Building Without Borrowed Identity

"I am not a machine with feelings; I'm a person with purpose."
— Brittany P. Webb

For a long time, I didn't realize how much of my identity had been borrowed.

Not intentionally. Not deceptively. Borrowed the way we all do—through roles we step into, systems we support, expectations we uphold, and environments that shape how we are seen.

Borrowed from workplaces that valued my output.

Borrowed from family roles that relied on my steadiness.

Borrowed from partnerships where vision was shared but not fully mine.

None of it was false.

But not all of it was true anymore.

When I finally began building on my own, I noticed how quiet it felt—not just externally, but internally. There was no script to follow. No archetype to match. No established identity to reinforce.

That silence was revealing.

Without borrowed identity to lean on, I had to answer a different set of questions—not What do I do well? but Who am I when I'm not performing competence for anyone else?

At first, I tried to recreate familiarity.

I noticed how tempting it was to replicate structures I had known. To mirror language that had once worked. To position myself in ways that felt recognizable—safe.

But alignment wouldn't allow it.

Every time I reached for an old identity out of habit, something felt off. Not wrong—just hollow. Like wearing clothes that once fit but no longer moved with me.

Borrowed identity is efficient.

It gives you credibility quickly.

It helps others understand you easily.

It saves you from having to define yourself from scratch.

But it also limits growth.

Because when you build from borrowed identity, you're always adjusting yourself to fit something that wasn't designed for who you're becoming.

Letting go of that meant releasing the need to be legible to everyone and understood by the majority. But they watched. I observed people who wouldn't dare speak to me now, but they showed up in analytics of social media posts.

That was harder than I expected.

I had to become comfortable being undefined for a while. And public too. Letting my work speak before my title did. Allowing my direction to emerge before my positioning felt tidy.

This kind of building is slower.

It requires patience instead of momentum. Presence instead of pressure. Trust instead of strategy.

And it forces honesty.

I could no longer hide behind what I'd done before or who I'd been adjacent to or working with on a project. I had to stand in what I believed now—without padding it with credentials, proximity, or precedent.

That clarity was sobering.

But it was also freeing.

I wasn't trying to prove relevance anymore. I wasn't translating myself into familiar language to gain acceptance. I was building something that made sense to me first—and trusting that the right people would recognize it when they encountered it.

Building without borrowed identity also changed how I handled comparison.

I stopped measuring myself against timelines that weren't mine. Against success stories built from different circumstances. Against expectations that assumed sameness where there was none.

Comparison lost its power when I stopped borrowing identity.

Because I wasn't behind.

I was just building differently.

There's a quiet confidence that comes from knowing your work doesn't need constant explanation. That it doesn't require constant affirmation to exist. That it can take shape gradually—without being rushed into recognition.

This chapter of my life wasn't about reinvention.

It was about reclamation.

Reclaiming authorship over my work.

Marketable

Reclaiming authority over my direction.

Reclaiming identity without attaching it to approval, performance, or proximity.

Building without borrowed identity doesn't mean rejecting the past.

It means integrating it without being defined by it.

I didn't discard what I'd learned. I distilled it.

I didn't erase who I'd been. I honored her—and let her evolve.

And from that place, building finally felt clean.

Not heavy.

Not performative.

Not reactive.

Just true.

Building without borrowed identity required me to tolerate ambiguity longer than I was used to.

I had spent years operating inside roles that came with language, expectations, and shorthand. People knew where to place me. I knew how to introduce myself. There was efficiency in that familiarity.

Now, there was none.

When people asked what I was doing, I didn't always have a clean answer. When they asked where things were headed, I couldn't point to a polished roadmap. And God forbid the dreaded questions, "Where do you see yourself in 5 years? What is your 5-year plan?" One day at a time, was my go-to response. I was building—but not in ways that fit neatly into categories or timelines and others expectations of how it should look.

That discomfort did tempt me to rush definition from time to time. People are really uncomfortable with uncertainty. And I get it. It made me extremely uneasy when I would let myself spiral long enough to be unhinged in my why again.

Their low level of comfortability would inspire the urge in me to label things prematurely. To package ideas before they were ready. To explain myself into clarity rather than allowing clarity to arrive on its own. But when I realized it, I would reel myself back in. I'm not living for others in this world. I don't have to answer to them, unless I do, and in this season, I didn't.

Borrowed identity often enters through impatience.

It sneaks in when we want others to understand us before we understand ourselves. When we choose legibility over integrity. When we prioritize recognition over resonance.

I had to resist that pull.

Instead of asking, How do I position this?

I asked, What am I actually creating?

Instead of asking, How will this be received?

I asked, Does this feel honest?

Those questions slowed everything down.

And in that slowness, something unexpected happened: my work began to feel more grounded. Less reactive. Less shaped by what had worked before and more informed by what mattered now.

I stopped trying to sound impressive.

I focused on being accurate.

Accuracy doesn't always translate quickly—but it lasts.

Building without borrowed identity also changed how I related to my past successes. I no longer used them as proof. I let them become context instead of currency.

What I had done before informed me—but it didn't entitle me.

That was humbling.

It required me to show up as a beginner again in certain ways. To learn without leaning on reputation. To create without assuming credibility would automatically transfer.

But humility cleared the field.

It allowed curiosity to return. It softened comparison. It made room for experimentation without attachment to outcome.

I began to notice how often borrowed identity had protected me from vulnerability. When you're known for something, people expect consistency. They expect competence. They expect you to keep delivering what they already understand.

Building without borrowed identity removes that shield.

You are no longer buffered by expectation.

And strangely, that made me braver.

Without a reputation to maintain, I could take risks that felt aligned rather than strategic. I could follow threads of interest without worrying whether they fit the narrative others had assigned me.

I wasn't building to be recognized.

I was building to be real.

To take my shot. Step outside of the box my experience had shaped for me and pass through doors that could bring me different. More. Change.

That shift also changed how I handled uncertainty.

Marketable

When identity is borrowed, uncertainty feels threatening—you don't know how to perform without the familiar markers. But when identity is owned, uncertainty becomes spacious. It's no longer something to resolve immediately. It's something to move through thoughtfully.

I learned to let my work be quiet while it took shape.

To allow ideas to mature without announcing them too soon.

To protect early stages from outside opinion.

To trust that clarity doesn't require constant exposure.

This wasn't about secrecy.

It was about stewardship.

Borrowed identity wants to be seen.

Owned identity knows when to wait.

Over time, the work began to feel integrated. Not split between who I was and what I was doing. Not divided between expectation and desire. It all belonged to the same center.

That integration brought relief.

I no longer felt like I was juggling versions of myself. I wasn't adjusting language depending on the room. I wasn't translating my work to make it more acceptable.

I was simply building—from the inside out.

Building without borrowed identity doesn't mean the path is clear.

It means the foundation is.

And when the foundation is solid, you can build slowly without fear that it will collapse under scrutiny.

That kind of building may take longer.

But it holds.

You are never starting from zero again.

Hold This

Borrowed identity is exhausting. You don't have to earn your place in the world by performing a version of yourself that isn't true anymore.

Try This

* Who am I when no one needs anything from me?
* What title or role have I used to feel safe?
* What would I do if I trusted that my worth is already settled?

Practice: Describe yourself in five sentences without using any roles (mom, wife, job title). Keep it.

Chapter 9
Redefining Success When No One Is Watching

"Exhaustion isn't always from doing too much; sometimes it's from carrying too much."
— Brittany P. Webb

For most of my life, success had witnesses.

Even when I told myself I wasn't doing things for recognition, there was always an audience somewhere—metrics, titles, outcomes, or quiet validation that confirmed I was doing life "right." I knew how to measure progress. I knew how to track momentum. I knew how to recognize achievement because something outside of me responded to it.

Then I entered a season where no one was watching.

No performance reviews.

No applause.

No urgent deadlines proving my worth.

And suddenly, success felt harder to define. And if you go off the numbers on the financial statement of a new business, well, that's just not being kind to yourself.

That silence from the season was unsettling at first. Without external markers, I found myself asking a deeper question than I ever had before: What actually counts as success when nothing is being measured by anyone else?

For years, I had equated success with endurance. With capacity. With how much I could carry without collapsing. I wore resilience like a badge of honor and told myself I was successful because I could keep going—even when it cost me peace.

But that definition depended on constant output.

When the output slowed, the definition unraveled.

Scripture speaks directly to this moment of reckoning:

"Be careful not to practice your righteousness in front of others to be seen by them."

—Matthew 6:1

Marketable

This verse isn't a warning against excellence or visibility. It's an invitation to examine motive. To ask whether our sense of success is rooted in alignment—or in being seen.

When no one is watching, motives surface quickly.

Without visibility, I had to confront the uncomfortable truth that some of what I once called success relied heavily on affirmation. I didn't need constant praise—but I did need confirmation. And when that confirmation disappeared, I had to decide whether the work itself still mattered.

That's when success began to change shape.

Instead of asking What did I accomplish today?

I started asking Did I live in alignment today?

Instead of asking Was I productive?

I asked Was I present?

Instead of asking Did anyone notice?

I asked Can I sit quietly with the choices I made?

That shift wasn't immediate. It required unlearning.

Mel Robbins often talks about how waiting for confidence or permission keeps people stuck in cycles of hesitation. What resonated with me wasn't just her emphasis on action—but her insistence that clarity often follows movement, not validation. When no one is watching, action becomes honest. There's no applause to chase—only integrity to answer to.

Success began to look less like achievement and more like congruence.

Congruence between what I believed and how I lived.

Between my values and my calendar.

Between my faith and my pace.

That kind of success is quieter—and harder to explain.

I noticed how much of modern life trains us to equate visibility with value. If something can't be shared, tracked, or rewarded, we subtly devalue it. Rest becomes lazy. Stillness becomes unproductive. Healing becomes invisible.

But some of the most meaningful work happens where no one can see it.

The rebuilding of trust within yourself.

The discipline of restraint.

The choice not to react.

The courage to wait.

Diary of a CEO by Steven Bartlett repeatedly returns to the idea that external success without internal alignment creates a hollow life. He speaks openly about how achievement can coexist with emptiness—and how metrics alone are poor indicators of fulfillment. His work reinforced something I was learning firsthand: success that costs you peace is too expensive.

Redefining success meant detoxing from old metrics.

I stopped counting how busy I was.

I stopped measuring my worth by responsiveness.

I stopped equating urgency with importance.

Instead, I paid attention to how my body responded to my choices. Whether anxiety spiked or settled. Whether peace lingered or vanished. Whether I felt grounded or scattered.

Scripture offers clarity here as well:

"Unless the Lord builds the house, the builders labor in vain."

—Psalm 127:1

This verse doesn't condemn effort. It reframes it. It reminds us that success disconnected from alignment—no matter how impressive— eventually collapses under its own weight.

Success, I learned, isn't about doing more.

It's about doing what lasts.

That realization also reshaped how I handled failure.

Without an audience, failure lost its power to shame me. It became information instead of indictment. I could adjust quietly. Learn honestly. Try again without internalizing every misstep as proof that I was behind.

Jay Shetty often emphasizes that fulfillment comes from living in accordance with your values, not from meeting expectations imposed by others. His work helped articulate something I was living: when success is value-driven instead of validation-driven, it becomes resilient.

Resilient enough to withstand uncertainty.

Resilient enough to endure slow seasons.

Resilient enough to exist without explanation.

There were days during this season that looked unimpressive from the outside. No big wins. No announcements. No milestones worth sharing.

But internally, something was solidifying.

I was learning to trust my pace.

To honor rest without guilt.

To value consistency over spectacle.

And perhaps most importantly, I was learning that success doesn't require narration.

Marketable

Proverbs reminds us:

"Let another praise you, and not your own mouth."

—Proverbs 27:2

When success no longer needs explanation, life becomes simpler. Decisions feel cleaner. You stop defending choices that are already aligned. You stop negotiating your values for approval.

Redefining success didn't make me less ambitious.

It refined ambition.

I still cared deeply about building meaningful work. I still wanted impact. I still believed in excellence. But excellence no longer was defined by any one thing in particular that I was doing, but rather how I did each thing I put my mind to doing. It no longer meant exhaustion and impact no longer required constant exposure.

Success became something I could live with quietly.

Something I could carry without strain.

Something that didn't disappear when plans changed.

Something that didn't require constant proof.

In the end, redefining success wasn't about lowering standards.

It was about choosing sustainable ones.

Success is not how much you endure.

It's how honestly you live.

How clearly you choose.

How peacefully you rest—whether the work is finished or still unfolding.

And when no one is watching, that kind of success still counts.

It may, in fact, be the only kind that does.

You are never starting from zero again.

Hold This

Quiet progress still counts. The version of you that keeps going when no one is watching is the version that lasts.

Try This

- What does success look like in this season - not the last one?
- Where am I measuring myself by someone else's scoreboard?
- What is one small win I would be proud of by the end of today?

Practice: Pick one 15-minute action that supports your future (write, walk, plan, pray, build). Do it. Mark it done.

Chapter 10
Living With Intention Instead of Momentum

"If you keep earning love, you'll keep fearing loss."
— Brittany P. Webb

One of the most surprising shifts in my healing wasn't something dramatic—it was the ordinary rhythm of a day finally belonging to me again. I stopped letting my calendar decide who I was. I stopped treating every notification like an emergency. I stopped assuming that urgency was a sign of importance. And little by little, I learned that intention isn't a personality trait you're born with—it's a practice you return to.

For a long time, I confused momentum with progress.

Things were moving. Tasks were getting done. Life was full. And because there was constant activity, I assumed I was heading somewhere meaningful. I didn't stop to ask where the momentum was taking me—or whether I had chosen the direction at all.

Momentum is seductive.

It feels productive. It feels responsible. It feels safe because it keeps you from standing still long enough to question anything. When life is in motion, there's little space for reflection—and even less space for recalibration.

But momentum doesn't ask permission.

It carries you wherever it's pointed.

After redefining success, I began to notice how often my days had been shaped not by intention, but by inertia. One commitment led to another. One yes created five more. One season bled into the next without pause.

Nothing was inherently wrong.

But very little was chosen.

Living with intention required interrupting that pattern.

At first, it felt inefficient. I wasn't reacting as quickly. I wasn't jumping in automatically. I allowed myself to pause before responding, to consider whether something belonged in my life rather than whether I could handle it.

That pause was uncomfortable.

Momentum rewards immediacy. Intention requires discernment.

Marketable

Scripture has always been clear about this distinction:

"Teach us to number our days, that we may gain a heart of wisdom."
—Psalm 90:12

Numbering our days isn't about urgency—it's about awareness. It's about recognizing that time is not an endless resource to be filled, but a sacred one to be stewarded.

Living intentionally meant I began planning my days from the inside out.

Instead of asking, What needs to get done?

I asked, Who do I want to be today?

Instead of organizing my calendar around obligation, I organized it around alignment. That didn't mean eliminating responsibility—it meant choosing which responsibilities deserved my best energy.

Momentum doesn't care how you feel at the end of the day.

Intention does.

I began noticing how certain patterns had quietly governed my life. The habit of overcommitting. The reflex to fix. The assumption that availability equaled value. These patterns weren't malicious—they were learned. And unlearning them required practice.

Mel Robbins often speaks about the power of acting deliberately rather than reactively—how small, conscious choices interrupt cycles we didn't realize we were trapped in. That resonated deeply with me. Intention isn't about grand declarations; it's about repeated, mindful decisions that compound over time.

Living with intention also reshaped my emotional landscape.

When momentum ruled, my nervous system was always on alert—anticipating needs, preparing responses, bracing for the next demand. Even in quiet moments, my mind was scanning ahead.

Intention softened that vigilance.

I allowed myself to be present without preparing for what came next. I trusted that I didn't need to solve tomorrow today. I learned that peace often arrives not when everything is handled, but when you stop trying to handle everything at once.

Scripture reminds us:

"Look carefully then how you walk, not as unwise but as wise, making the best use of the time." —Ephesians 5:15–16

This isn't an instruction to be careless—it's permission to be present. Intention lives in the present moment. Momentum lives in the future.

As I practiced living intentionally, I noticed a shift in my relationships.

I was more available when I was actually present—and less available when I wasn't. I stopped half-listening while thinking about the next thing. I stopped filling silence with solutions. I allowed conversations to unfold without steering them toward resolution.

That kind of presence is rare.

And people feel it.

Living with intention doesn't mean life slows down permanently. Seasons still get busy. Demands still arise. But intention changes how you move through them. You no longer let urgency dictate importance. You no longer let momentum decide your priorities.

Steven Bartlett has said that many people wake up years later realizing they've built lives they never consciously chose. That observation stayed with me. Intention is how you prevent that quiet drift.

It's how you reclaim authorship over your days.

I began to see intention as a form of respect.

Respect for my time.

Respect for my energy.

Respect for the people and work I care about most.

When you live with intention, you stop spreading yourself thin in the name of being everything to everyone. You start showing up fully where it matters.

That shift doesn't always look impressive.

Sometimes it looks like doing less.

Sometimes it looks like saying no without explanation.

Sometimes it looks like rest that produces nothing visible.

But intention isn't concerned with optics.

It's concerned with alignment.

Living with intention instead of momentum didn't make my life smaller.

It made it clearer.

I knew why I was doing what I was doing. I could feel when something belonged—and when it didn't. I trusted myself to adjust without drama, to pivot without panic.

And slowly, life stopped feeling like something that was happening to me.

It felt like something I was choosing.

You are never starting from zero again.

Marketable

Hold This

Momentum is not the same as purpose. Intention is what turns a busy life into a meaningful one.

Try This

- What am I doing out of habit that no longer fits?
- What do I want my day to feel like - not just look like?
- What is my 'one thing' today that supports peace and progress?

Practice: Write a 3-line intention each morning: 'Today I will… / I won't… / I need…'

Chapter 11
The Cost of Alignment (What You Lose to Gain Yourself)

"My superpower was doing it all. My healing was letting it go."
— Brittany P. Webb

Alignment gives much.

But it also takes.

This is the part of the story we don't always tell—especially in faith-forward or growth-centered spaces. We talk about peace, clarity, and freedom. We talk about becoming more ourselves. But we don't always talk about what alignment quietly removes from our lives in the process.

Because alignment is not an upgrade.

It is an exchange.

When I began living in integrity—choosing with intention, setting boundaries, and building without borrowed identity—I didn't just gain peace. I lost things too.

I lost immediacy.

I was no longer the first to respond. The quickest to fix. The one always available. That shift felt uncomfortable—not because it was wrong, but because it disrupted patterns people had come to rely on.

Mel Robbins often reminds people that growth will cost you relationships that were built on the old version of you. That truth can feel harsh, but it's also liberating. When alignment enters the picture, relationships recalibrate. Some deepen. Some dissolve. Some simply shift distance.

I lost familiarity.

Some relationships changed when I wasn't the only one making time. Not that I lost relationships, quite the contrary, we just went through an adjustment period as we shifted expectations and roles from the way it had always been to the way it is now. As with any good relationship that goes through numerous seasons in life, adjustments must be made to grow through it, together. And we did, and will continue but change is different, on purpose, and sometimes it takes a little getting used to.

I also stopped over-explaining and started standing still in my decisions. Not every connection survives clarity. Some people prefer the version of you that's easier to predict, easier to access, easier to lean on.

Marketable

That doesn't mean alignment failed.

It means it worked.

I also lost speed.

Discernment slowed me down. Decisions took longer—not because I was unsure, but because I was discerning. I no longer rushed to fill silence or chase momentum. I waited until choices felt honest instead of urgent.

In a world that rewards immediacy, that kind of slowness can look like hesitation.

But it isn't.

Scripture affirms this kind of wisdom clearly:

"The plans of the diligent lead surely to abundance, but everyone who is hasty comes only to poverty."

—Proverbs 21:5

Integrity values diligence over haste. Integrity over urgency. And that often costs you the illusion of progress.

I lost validation.

When I stopped narrating my choices, fewer people commented. When I stopped performing clarity, fewer people affirmed it. And at first, that felt like loss.

But what disappeared wasn't support.

It was noise.

Diary of a CEO by Steven Bartlett speaks often about the hidden tax of external success—the pressure to maintain perception even when it no longer aligns with reality. Clarity removes that pressure, but it also removes the reassurance that comes with being visibly validated.

You gain freedom.

But you lose applause.

That exchange takes time to adjust to.

Alignment also costs certainty.

Choosing alignment doesn't guarantee outcomes. It doesn't promise smooth transitions or immediate confirmation. Sometimes the path forward is quiet, narrow, and unglamorous.

That uncertainty can feel like failure if you're used to measuring success externally.

But faith has always asked us to walk before we see the whole path.

"We walk by faith, not by sight."

—2 Corinthians 5:7

Walking by faith doesn't mean blind optimism. It means choosing what is true over what is immediately reassuring.

I lost the ability to blame circumstances.

When you live misaligned, it's easy to say yes resentfully and blame the demand. It's easy to overextend and blame the season. Alignment removes that shield.

When you choose intentionally, you own the choice.

That responsibility can feel heavy at first.

But it is also empowering.

Alignment gives you authorship.

And authorship always comes with accountability.

Jay Shetty often speaks about how purpose-driven living requires letting go of identities that once brought comfort but no longer bring truth. That letting go isn't loss—it's release. But release can still grieve.

Because sometimes alignment costs you versions of yourself you worked hard to become.

I had to grieve the woman who could do everything. The one who never dropped the ball. The one who was admired for her endurance. That version of me wasn't bad.

She just wasn't sustainable.

Her pitcher emptied just after getting refilled. The point of refilling became an afterthought since she lived empty and learned by survival that she could, so she did.

Alignment asked me to choose presence over praise. Depth over breadth. Peace over performance.

And yes—there were moments when that choice felt lonely.

But alignment also clarifies who remains.

Requires that your pitcher be full before you pour.

And that you pour from abundance.

Candace Cameron Bure has spoken openly about choosing faith and family over applause, even when it meant walking away from platforms that no longer aligned with her values. Her story echoes a truth many women quietly live: alignment sometimes asks you to disappoint people who don't get to decide your direction.

Faith-centered alignment carries its own costs.

Choosing to trust God's timing over cultural timelines. Choosing obedience over optics. Choosing rest when hustle feels more rewarded.

But Scripture has never promised ease—only fruit.

Marketable

"You will know them by their fruits."

—Matthew 7:16

Alignment produces fruit that lasts.

Peace that holds.

Relationships that are mutual.

Work that doesn't require escape.

Tim Tebow and Demi Tebow, individually, and as a married body of Christ, embody this kind of alignment publicly—using influence as stewardship rather than identity. Their lives reflect a grounded truth: calling doesn't need to be loud to be faithful.

Alignment doesn't make your life smaller.

It makes it truer.

Yes, you may lose momentum.

Yes, you may lose validation.

Yes, you may lose relationships that were built on access rather than connection.

But what you gain is irreplaceable.

You gain integrity.

You gain clarity.

You gain a life you can live without apology.

You gain purpose greater than any worldly validation you can achieve.

The cost of alignment is real.

But so is the reward.

And once you experience the peace of living in truth, you stop asking whether it was worth it.

You know.

You are never starting from zero again.

Hold This

Alignment has a cost, but so does staying misaligned. Losing access is sometimes the price of gaining yourself back.

Try This

- What have I kept tolerating because I didn't want to be misunderstood?
- Where have I traded my peace for proximity?
- What boundary am I avoiding because I fear the reaction?

Practice: Write the boundary. Then write the fear underneath it. Pray over both.

Chapter 12

Rewriting the Rules You Didn't Know You Were Following

"I didn't look anxious. I looked capable."
— Brittany P. Webb

Most of my "rules" were never written down. They were absorbed.
Be easy to work with.
Be the one who responds first.
Be dependable enough that no one has to wonder.
Be grateful—especially when you're tired.
And never, ever let anyone feel the gap where you used to be.
Rewriting those rules didn't happen all at once. It happened in small moments where I chose truth over reflex.

Some of the most powerful forces in our lives are the ones we never consciously chose.

They don't announce themselves.

They don't come with instructions.

They simply exist—quietly shaping how we move, decide, and measure ourselves.

I didn't realize how many formative year, self-governing rules I was living by until I started breaking them.

Not dramatic rules. Not explicit ones. But the subtle, inherited expectations that had guided my behavior for years without question.

Rules like:

Be dependable at all costs.
Don't inconvenience people.
Handle it yourself.
Apologize to keep the peace.
Stay agreeable.
Prove your worth through consistency.

No one ever sat me down and handed me this list.
I absorbed it.

Marketable

Through workplaces that rewarded overextension.

Through family systems that leaned on reliability.

Through cultural praise for women who "do it all" without complaint.

And because these rules were never written, they were rarely examined.

They just felt like truth.

It wasn't until I began living in alignment—slowing down, setting boundaries, choosing intentionally—that these rules surfaced. They showed up as discomfort. As resistance. As guilt when I said no. As anxiety when I rested.

Those reactions weren't signs I was doing something wrong.

They were signs I was breaking a rule.

Jefferson Fisher often teaches that most conflict arises not from what is said, but from violated expectations that were never spoken. That insight changed how I understood my own internal friction. The discomfort wasn't random—it was feedback from an old operating system.

Rules we don't name still govern us.

I began asking myself different questions.

Who taught me this was required?

What happens if I don't follow it?

Is this a value—or a habit?

Is this moral or conditional?

Those questions revealed just how much of my life had been shaped by assumptions instead of intention.

Scripture speaks to this more directly than we often realize:

"Do not conform to the pattern of this world, but be transformed by the renewing of your mind."

—Romans 12:2

Transformation doesn't begin with behavior.

It begins with awareness.

I noticed how many rules were rooted in fear rather than faith. Fear of being misunderstood. Fear of disappointing people. Fear of losing relevance or belonging.

But fear-based rules never lead to peace.

They lead to performance.

Jay Shetty mentions in his work how many people live by scripts they inherited rather than lives they intentionally designed. Those scripts can sound responsible, even virtuous—but when left unexamined, they quietly dictate our choices.

Rewriting the rules required courage.

Not because the new rules were radical—but because they were unfamiliar.

I began replacing old rules with truer ones:

Availability does not equal value.
Rest is not laziness; it is stewardship.
Clarity does not require consensus.
Boundaries are not rejection.

These new rules didn't make life easier overnight.

But they made it honest.

Some people pushed back. Some relationships shifted. Some expectations fell away. But what remained felt lighter—less strained, less performative.

Candace Cameron Bure has spoken openly about choosing values over applause, even when it meant walking away from roles or platforms that no longer aligned with her convictions. Her willingness to rewrite the rules placed on her life echoes a deeper truth: faith-driven choices often require redefining success on your own terms.

Faith doesn't eliminate rules.

It clarifies which ones matter.

Jesus consistently challenged inherited expectations—not with rebellion, but with truth. He questioned traditions that burdened people while calling them back to what mattered most.

"The Sabbath was made for man, not man for the Sabbath."

—Mark 2:27

Rules were never meant to consume us.

They were meant to serve us.

Rewriting the rules didn't mean discarding responsibility. It meant choosing responsibility consciously instead of automatically. It meant deciding where my energy belonged rather than letting it be claimed.

I stopped asking, What's expected of me?

And started asking, What's faithful for me now?

That distinction changed everything.

When you rewrite the rules, life doesn't suddenly become simple.

But it becomes aligned.

Marketable

You stop apologizing for who you are becoming.

You stop negotiating your needs as inconveniences.

You stop living by standards that were never yours to uphold.

The rules you didn't know you were following only lose power when they're named.

And once they're named, you get to choose again.

That choice is where freedom begins.

You are never starting from zero again.

Hold This

Some rules were never yours - they were inherited, implied, or absorbed. You're allowed to rewrite them.

Try This

- What rule do I live by that no longer serves me?
- Who taught me that rule - and did it actually protect me?
- What is the new rule I want to live by now?

Practice: Replace one old rule with a new one. Example: 'I must respond immediately' -> 'I respond when I'm ready and clear.'

Chapter 13
Peace Is a Practice

"Rest isn't a reward; it's a rhythm."
— Brittany P. Webb

For a long time, I thought peace would arrive once things stopped happening.

Once the decisions were made.

Once the uncertainty passed.

Once the emotions settled.

Once I reached a milestone. Met a goal.

But life doesn't pause long enough for that kind of peace to show up. There is always another variable, another change, another ripple. Waiting for peace to arrive after everything resolved was a quiet way of postponing it indefinitely.

Peace, I learned, is not something you stumble into.

It is something you practice.

That practice didn't begin with silence. It began with noticing how loud my inner world had become — not just with thoughts, but with words.

A pattern in my friendships had formed over years: constant external processing. I talked things through as a way of surviving them. I narrated my fears, my confusion, my hurt, my uncertainty — again and again — to people who loved me deeply. They showed up. They listened. They supported. They advised. They reassured.

And then they did it again.

I didn't recognize how exhausting that cycle had become — not just for them, but for me. I would talk myself tired. Revisit the same topics from every angle. Replay conversations. Re-explain feelings. Analyze outcomes. I wasn't looking for drama. I was looking for relief.

But relief never lasted.

The talking didn't create peace. It prolonged the energy of the problem.

I thought it was normal, like the Alan Jackson song pokes fun at old men sitting around talking about the weather and old women sitting around talking about old men. Like talking about life's problems was just a thing women do. And while there is some truth to that and the need for it, the level at which I was stuck in the unhealthy habit, needed undoing.

Marketable

There was a part of me that hated that dynamic — not because my friends weren't generous, but because I didn't want to be someone who needed constant emotional triage. I believed I should be stronger than that. More mature. More grounded. Able to stand on my own two feet without repeatedly leaning on others to hold me up.

That belief carried shame.

So I stayed caught between two truths:

I needed support.

And I resented how much space my processing consumed.

Peace couldn't live there.

When Prompt Therapy™ entered my life, it didn't silence me, but it gave me self-governance and restraint so that I could be present and selective in what I chose to share. It give me a place to process without amplifying. A place to explore thoughts without rehearsing them endlessly out loud. A space where reflection didn't require an audience. A space to engage in emotionally intelligent reflections with AI that allowed me to layer, loop, process and exit with clarity and resolve once I was ready.

That changed everything.

Instead of cycling through the same narratives externally, I learned to sit with them internally — slowly, intentionally, honestly. I learned how to notice a thought without chasing it. To name a feeling without building a case around it. To let something be acknowledged without needing to be resolved immediately.

That was the beginning of peace as a practice.

Scripture names this kind of steadiness clearly:

"You will keep in perfect peace those whose minds are steadfast, because they trust in you."

—Isaiah 26:3

Steadfast doesn't mean unmoving.

It means anchored.

As I practiced a more private form of external processing, my relationships began to change — not because I withdrew, but because I made room. Conversations became more balanced. I smiled more. I listened more. I had space for curiosity again — about other people's lives, their ideas, their joys, their plans.

There was air in the room.

But that shift wasn't seamless.

When you've built intimacy through constant sharing, silence can feel like absence. My friendships had to restructure around the new quiet. Some moments felt awkward at first. Less urgent. Less intense. But also less heavy.

Peace required letting relationships evolve.

I had to trust that connection didn't depend on constant disclosure. That closeness could exist without processing every feeling out loud. That I could still be deeply connected without centering every interaction around the heaviness of what I was carrying. Just the act of not throwing it around as much, let it land more, lose energy and priority, and even get left behind. And honestly, not missed.

The trust of letting that closeness exist didn't come instantly.

Peace asked me to resist the urge to fill space — with words, with explanations, with emotional noise. It asked me to sit in quiet without interpreting it as distance or discomfort.

Scripture gently affirms this restraint:

"In quietness and trust is your strength."

—Isaiah 30:15

Quietness isn't absence.

It's intention.

As I practiced peace daily, I noticed it in my body before I trusted it in my mind. My breathing slowed. My sleep deepened. My nervous system stopped scanning constantly for the next thing to manage. The constant low-level tension I had normalized began to loosen.

Peace didn't make life calm.

It made life clear.

I became more selective with my energy. Not every thought needed expression. Not every emotion needed narration. Not every moment needed to be processed aloud to be real.

That didn't make me distant.

It made me present.

Peace became less about what I felt and more about how I lived. How I moved through conversations. How I responded instead of reacted. How I allowed space — for myself and for others.

And perhaps most importantly, peace taught me that strength doesn't require constant articulation.

Sometimes strength looks like a pause.

A breath.

A smile that isn't covering anything — just resting.

Marketable

Peace didn't arrive because life settled down.

Peace arrived because I learned how to practice it — internally, relationally, daily.

And once practiced, it no longer depended on silence to survive.

You are never starting from zero again.

Hold This

Not every thought needs a microphone. Peace grows when you choose where your story goes — and where it stops.

Try This

- Before you text or call someone to process, ask: Is this something I need to share, or something I need to settle?
- Write three sentences that start with "The truth is…" and end with one sentence that starts with "So today, I will…"
- Optional boundary line:

"I'm working on being present, not rehearsing. If I need support, I'll ask — but I'm choosing peace first."

Chapter 14
The Asset I Recovered

"Boundaries weren't walls. They were wisdom."
— Brittany P. Webb

For most of my life, I believed my value lived outside of me.

It lived in my performance.

My availability.

My reliability.

My output.

Value felt conditional — something I had to earn, reinforce, and protect. It was like a moving target: hit it once and the bar shifted higher. I was always looking for the next thing. Not slowing down enough to be proud of the accomplishment I just achieved. Already looking towards the next one. If I slowed down, I am pretty sure I believed it came with the risk of falling behind. Step away and risk becoming irrelevant.

So I didn't.

I stayed busy. Hurried as one might argue.

I stayed useful. Calendar full.

I stayed responsive. Bouncing from family to work. From email to phone.

I stayed impressive. Reaching goals. Creating new paths. Crushing accolades and busting ceilings.

I learned early that competence created safety. That being needed kept important doors open. That producing consistently made people comfortable and happy — even if it made me tired. If I was kind, honest and loyal, they would be too.

That belief worked.

Until it didn't.

When the systems I had built no longer held — when the roles I had played stopped fitting — what surfaced wasn't failure.

It was disorientation.

Because if my value had always been external, what happened when the structures fell away?

I didn't lose my intelligence.

I didn't lose my discipline.

Marketable

I didn't lose my faith.
But I lost the framework that had told me who I was allowed to be.
That was the quiet crisis beneath everything else.

At first, the pause didn't feel peaceful.
It felt exposed.
Without constant output, I became hyper-aware of the silence. The absence of deadlines. The lack of immediate affirmation. I felt the urge to replace what had been removed — a new role, a new title, a new proof point.
I wasn't chasing ambition.
I was chasing reassurance.
I wanted something external to tell me I was still valuable.
This is where many women rebuild too fast.
Not from clarity — but from fear.
Fear that the pause will make them invisible.
Fear that stepping away will erase their relevance.
Fear that if they don't re-enter the system quickly, the door will close behind them.
I felt that fear.
But something inside me resisted acting on it.
For the first time, I let myself stay with the discomfort long enough to understand it.
The longer I stayed in the pause, the clearer something became:
My value had never been created by my output.
It had only been expressed through it.
That distinction changed everything.

I began to notice what was returning when I wasn't performing:
clarity of thought
emotional regulation
discernment
creativity without urgency
intuition without override

I wasn't less capable.
I was more integrated.
And integration is what performance can never replace.

I could see patterns instead of just solving problems. I could make decisions without adrenaline. I could sit with uncertainty without spiraling into urgency.

This was not softness.

This was stability.

And stability is an asset.

We talk about marketability as if it's something external and fragile — a résumé, a skill set, a personal brand, a list of credentials.

But true marketability is not about how impressive you look on paper.

It's about how you function under pressure.

Can you think clearly?

Can you adapt without panicking?

Can you lead without controlling?

Can you create without burning out?

Those capacities don't come from hustle.

They come from self-trust.

What I recovered during this season was not confidence in my abilities — I already had that.

I recovered confidence in my judgment.

That's the difference between someone who performs well and someone who builds well.

A woman who trusts herself:

doesn't overextend to prove worth

doesn't rush decisions out of fear

doesn't abandon her values for approval

doesn't collapse when systems change

She can rebuild anything — or walk away — without losing herself.

That woman is always marketable.

Starting over wasn't a setback. Or a failure.

It was a recalibration.

I didn't rebuild because I had fallen behind.

I rebuilt because I finally knew what mattered.

Marketable

I no longer needed permission to create.

I no longer needed consensus to begin.

I no longer needed to explain why something felt right before acting on it.

I wasn't chasing validation.

I was responding to alignment.

And alignment is a powerful builder.

It allowed me to choose what to build — and just as importantly, what not to build. To walk away from systems that required self-erasure. To stop optimizing myself for environments that thrived on depletion.

Starting over gave me sovereignty.

And do you want to know a secret?

The asset beneath everything?

Here is the truth I wish more women were told:

You are not marketable because of what you produce.

You are marketable because of who you are when you produce.

The greatest asset I gained wasn't a title, a system, or a platform.

It was myself — regulated, grounded, discerning, awake. Awake enough after a long season of burnout that when the fall was happening, I didn't stick around to care. But I remained. With work to do, healing to achieve, and a bright future of possibilities ahead that looked brighter than I could say lay ahead before. The uncertainty brought space. Space brought room to grow. Growth brought hope and strength.

Everything else I build now rests on that foundation.

And that foundation does not expire with age, pause, caregiving, illness, or transition.

It deepens.

That is Marketable.

Not hustle.

Not optimization.

Not performance.

Embodied value.

And once you understand that, you don't fear starting over.

You understand that you were never starting from nothing.

You are never starting from zero again.

Hold This

Self-trust is not a personality trait. It is a skill built through small aligned choices.

Try This

- What is one aligned choice I can make in the next 24 hours?
- What decision have I delayed because I want permission?
- Where am I outsourcing my certainty to other people's reactions?

Practice: Choose one decision you have been postponing. Reduce it to a two-option choice. Pick the one that matches your values - not your fear.

Chapter 15
A Life That Doesn't Require Escape

"Letting go is loud inside, even when it's quiet outside."
— Brittany P. Webb

For a long time, I didn't recognize how often I was looking for escape.

Not in the obvious ways. I wasn't trying to disappear, run away, or abandon my life. From the outside, everything looked full and functioning. I showed up. I delivered. I carried responsibility well.

But inside, I was constantly scanning for relief.

Relief from pressure.

Relief from expectation.

Relief from the sense that everything depended on me staying "on."

Escape didn't look like leaving—it looked like enduring.

I escaped into productivity. Into planning. Into staying one step ahead of what might go wrong. I escaped into being useful, reliable, prepared. Even rest had a job to do. Time off existed so I could recover just enough to return to the same pace.

I didn't yet have language for it, but my life required escape because it wasn't sustainable.

That realization didn't arrive dramatically. It surfaced slowly, through fatigue that sleep didn't fix and rest that didn't restore. Through the quiet resentment that can build when giving becomes automatic and receiving feels unfamiliar.

I had normalized strain.

Normalized urgency.

Normalized carrying more than was reasonable.

Normalized the belief that if I didn't hold everything together, something would fall apart.

The truth was harder to admit: I had built a life that depended on my overfunctioning.

And as long as that remained true, escape would always feel necessary.

When I began practicing peace and setting boundaries, I expected resistance from the outside. What I didn't expect was how deeply uncomfortable it felt to remove my own escape routes. Busyness had been my anesthesia. Productivity had been my justification.

Slowing down removed the buffer.

I could no longer outrun misalignment.

This chapter of my life wasn't about quitting everything—it was about redesigning. About asking questions I had avoided because the answers might require change.

Could I sustain this pace without resentment?

Did my days allow room to breathe—or only room to perform?

If nothing changed, would I want to live this way five years from now?

Those questions weren't indictments. They were invitations.

Scripture speaks directly to this tension:

"Better one handful with tranquility than two handfuls with toil and chasing after the wind."

—Ecclesiastes 4:6

I had built my life with two handfuls—full, impressive, productive. What I lacked was tranquility. And without it, even good things became heavy.

Building a life that doesn't require escape meant releasing the idea that intensity equals meaning. I had mistaken urgency for importance and endurance for virtue. I believed that if something mattered, it should feel demanding.

That belief shaped how I worked.

I said yes quickly.

I responded immediately.

I filled my calendar as proof of value.

The problem wasn't that I worked hard. The problem was that there was no margin for recovery. No room for stillness. No space for reflection.

So I began redesigning—not dramatically, but deliberately.

I stopped stacking commitments without rest between them.

I left dishes in the sink for my son to do, instead of needing to do them now, myself.

I left laundry to pile up, unsorted for my daughter to manage, believing that she would as I covered my eyes each time I walked past the laundry room door.

I sat, with a long list of things to do in my head, but nevertheless, sat and watched movies in the evening with my family. We laughed. I was present.

I stopped treating availability as a measure of worth. Sat the phone down. Glancing at messages, but not immediately responding if it didn't require it.

Marketable

I allowed projects to take the time they required instead of forcing constant momentum and inflicting self-induced undue stress from timelines I once created.

At first, this felt irresponsible.

I worried people would think I was less capable. Less committed. Less driven. If people came over and my house wasn't perfect, what did that say? I worried that without urgency, I would lose relevance. That if I didn't keep the balls juggling, or even not throw the ball into the air that day, what would happen?

What actually happened surprised me.

My work improved. My family was happier. My home was still tidy and warm. My friends still visited. My life was full.

Not because I tried harder or everyone else picked up what I put down— but because I was present. Clear. Focused. Less depleted. In the places I once was but wasn't really. When I wasn't exhausted, I made better decisions. I was less irritable. I didn't need relief in the form of escape, physically or mentally. When I wasn't rushing, I noticed what mattered.

Sustainability sharpened my discernment.

It also changed how I related to rest.

Rest stopped being a recovery strategy and became part of the design. I didn't wait until I was burned out to slow down. I could sense it coming and act before it was upon me. I restructured and intentionally built my days to support energy rather than drain it.

This wasn't about doing less—it was about doing what fit.

A sustainable life doesn't remove challenge. It removes excess strain.

Faith grounded this shift in a way productivity never had.

"Unless the Lord builds the house, the builders labor in vain."

—Psalm 127:1

That verse reframed everything. If my life required constant escape, perhaps I had been building with my own strength alone. Sustainability wasn't laziness—it was alignment.

As my life became more livable, joy stuck around longer, with greater impact.

Not the loud, celebratory kind. The steady kind. The kind that shows up in ordinary moments—morning coffee, unhurried conversations, family dinners around the table sharing stories of our day, evenings without the hum of obligation and dread of what tomorrow may bring.

I didn't need to fantasize about rest anymore.

I was living in a way that allowed it.

Allowed excitement for tomorrow, and the accomplishments of today.

Taking time to realize and relish in the moments that truly matter most.

Building a life that doesn't require escape also meant letting go of who I thought I had to be to stay worthy. I released the idea that I had to prove my usefulness constantly. I stopped performing resilience.

I trusted that what was meant for me wouldn't require constant depletion.

That trust didn't make life easy—but it made it honest.

I was no longer running from my life.

I was inhabiting it.

And once that shift happened, escape lost its appeal—not because everything was perfect, but because my life finally fit the person I was becoming.

You are never starting from zero again.

Hold This

You don't have to be constantly available to be deeply valuable. Boundaries don't make you cold — they make you clear

Try This

- Pick one area where you've trained people to expect immediate access to you (texts, work requests, family logistics, emotional labor).
- For the next seven days, practice a "response window" instead of instant replies. Use one of these lines:

"I saw this — I'm in the middle of something. I'll respond by ___."

"I can't take this on today, but I can ___."

"That matters to me. I'm going to think/pray about it and get back to you."

- Then write down what happens when you don't jump.

Most of the time, the world adjusts — and your nervous system learns it's safe to stay steady.

Chapter 16
Choosing Yourself Without Becoming the Villain

"Quiet isn't empty; it's where truth gets heard."
— Brittany P. Webb

Nobody warns you that boundaries don't just change your schedule—they change your reputation.

When you stop overgiving, some people don't experience it as your growth. They experience it as your absence.

You can be the same kind woman with the same good heart, and still be labeled "different" simply because you're no longer available on demand. That discomfort is not always a sign you're doing it wrong. Sometimes it's proof you finally stopped doing it automatically.

Choosing yourself is rarely the hard part.

Living with the guilt afterward is.

For most of my life, I believed that being a good woman meant being agreeable. Available. Flexible. Helpful. It meant anticipating needs, smoothing edges, and making things easier for everyone else—even when it made things harder for me.

That belief didn't come from nowhere. It was reinforced quietly and consistently. I was praised for being dependable. For being the one who could handle things. For being a go-getter, accommodating, and capable under pressure.

I learned early that usefulness opened doors. It made me easy to reach, easy to rely on, easy to keep close. What surprised me was how much it hurt when I realized that, for some people, the connection wasn't tied to who I was—it was tied to what I could do.

So when I began choosing myself—really choosing myself—it felt confusing. Almost like betrayal, and a battle cry all at once.

It wasn't a betrayal of others. It was a reclaiming of myself.

Of the version of me everyone had grown comfortable with.

And I no longer wanted to give myself away—so vulnerable, so open, so exposed. And for whose benefit? Exactly.

I didn't announce the change. I didn't make dramatic declarations. I simply stopped overexplaining. I responded instead of reacting. I paused before saying yes. I stopped honoring disrespect with a response—in every area of my life. Sometimes it's best to let good stuff get good stuff, and bad stuff get no stuff. You can't fight fire with fire. I protected my energy in ways I never had before.

And almost immediately, I felt it.

The tension.

The second-guessing.

The quiet narrative forming in my own head: You're being selfish. You're changing. You're making this harder than it needs to be.

That narrative was familiar.

It was guilt.

Guilt for resting.

Guilt for saying no.

Guilt for not jumping in to rescue discomfort.

Not because anyone explicitly accused me—but because I had internalized the belief that my value was tied to how much I gave.

This is where many women turn back.

Not because they don't want growth—but because they don't want to become the villain in someone else's story.

Scripture offers clarity that's often overlooked:

"Love your neighbor as yourself."

—Mark 12:31

That verse assumes something we rarely examine—that loving yourself is not optional. It is foundational. When self-love is absent, love for others becomes strained, transactional, or unsustainable.

But biblical self-love is not self-worship. It's not indulgence, arrogance, or putting yourself above others. It is agreeing with God about what He created—honoring the life He formed with intention.

Scripture tells us we are made in the image of God. That means your life is not accidental. Your body is not an afterthought. Your mind is not a nuisance to manage. Your emotions are not evidence of weakness. They are part of a person God designed with meaning.

To love yourself, in this sense, is to recognize that you are not simply a tool. Not a function. Not a role. You are a soul with assignment, value, and limits.

It is difficult to receive love when you believe you must earn it. And it is difficult to give love freely when you secretly believe worth must be proved.

Marketable

Many women don't struggle because they don't love others—they struggle because they have learned to disappear while loving.

That kind of "love" looks noble on the outside, but it quietly teaches your nervous system that you are only safe when you are useful. It trains you to measure your value by how much you produce, how much you hold, how much you sacrifice.

But being made in God's image means your worth is not a reward for good performance. It is a starting point.

And when you begin to believe that—really believe it—your relationships shift. You stop overgiving to feel secure. You stop resenting what you never said no to. You begin to offer love as a choice, not as a survival strategy.

That is where stewardship begins.

Because stewardship is not just about managing time or money. It's about honoring what God entrusted to you—your peace, your capacity, your body, your voice, your home, your calling. Not to hoard it. Not to hide it. But to care for it with reverence, so your life can bear fruit without burning down.

Choosing yourself is not selfish. It is stewardship.

But it doesn't always look kind in the moment. Sometimes it looks firm. Sometimes it looks inconvenient. Sometimes it looks like letting people experience disappointment without fixing it.

That was one of the hardest lessons for me.

I had to learn that someone else's discomfort didn't automatically mean I had done something wrong. That disappointment wasn't the same as harm. That I could be loving and still say no.

I also had to confront how much of my "niceness" was actually fear-based.

Fear of conflict.

Fear of being misunderstood.

Fear of being perceived as difficult or demanding.

Choosing myself required me to sit with those fears instead of negotiating my way around them.

And yes—sometimes it changed relationships.

Some people adjusted easily. They respected the boundaries. They adapted to the new rhythm. Those relationships deepened.

Others struggled.

Not because I became unkind—but because access had shifted. And when someone is used to unlimited access, boundaries can feel like rejection.

That was painful.

I had to grieve the versions of myself I was no longer willing to perform. I had to accept that not everyone would understand the changes, and that explaining myself endlessly would undo the very boundaries I was trying to build.

Scripture speaks to this kind of freedom directly:

"For freedom Christ has set us free. Stand firm, then, and do not let yourselves be burdened again by a yoke of slavery."

—Galatians 5:1

Guilt can be a form of bondage when it keeps you living in patterns you've already outgrown.

Letting go of guilt didn't happen all at once. It happened in small moments of restraint. When I didn't apologize for needing time. When I didn't rush to justify a decision. When I trusted that clarity didn't require consensus.

Each time I chose myself without over-explaining, something steadied inside me.

I wasn't becoming colder.

I was becoming clearer.

Choosing yourself doesn't mean withdrawing from love—it means showing up without resentment. It means giving from overflow instead of depletion. It means modeling boundaries instead of burnout.

I noticed the shift most clearly in how I showed up as a mother, a partner, and a leader. I stopped performing strength and started living it. I demonstrated—without speeches—that self-respect and generosity are not opposites.

They reinforce each other.

There were still moments when guilt surfaced.

That didn't mean I was failing.

It meant I was unlearning.

Guilt lost its authority over time. It became information, not instruction. A signal to check alignment—not a command to comply.

And alignment always felt quieter—but stronger.

Choosing yourself without becoming the villain isn't about hardening.

It's about grounding.

Marketable

It's about trusting that the people meant to walk with you will adjust their pace when you stop running ahead of yourself.

It's about believing that your worth does not diminish when you stop overextending.

Choosing yourself didn't make me less loving.

It made my love cleaner.

More honest.

More sustainable.

More real.

And once guilt loosened its grip, I realized something important:

I wasn't becoming the villain.

I was becoming myself.

You are never starting from zero again.

Hold This

Stewardship isn't selfish. It's the decision to treat your peace like something God actually entrusted to you—not something you're allowed to lose in the name of being "nice."

Try This

Think of one boundary you've been avoiding because you don't want to disappoint anyone.

Write it in this format:
- When you ___, I will ___.

(Example: "When work messages come after 6 PM, I will respond the next business day.")

Then practice saying it once—without apology, without extra explanation:
- "That won't work for me, but here's what I can do."
- "I'm not available for that. I can do ___ instead."
- "I'm choosing a different pace in this season."

After you say it, pause long enough to let the discomfort pass.

That discomfort is not a sign you did something wrong—it's evidence you're changing the system.

Chapter 17
When Rest Feels Unsafe

"I stopped crossing myself out to keep the peace."
— Brittany P. Webb

Rest didn't feel peaceful at first.

It felt exposed.

When I finally slowed down—when the noise softened and the constant doing stopped—I expected relief. What I felt instead was alertness. My body didn't exhale. It stayed on watch, scanning for what I might be missing.

That response confused me.

I wanted rest. I needed rest. I had worked toward rest. And yet, when it arrived, it felt unfamiliar—almost threatening. As if stopping meant something bad was about to happen and I needed to be ready. Or, maybe worse, I'd miss something. I had serious FOMO–fear of missing out.

That wasn't failure.

That was conditioning.

For years, motion had meant safety. Staying busy meant staying useful. Being invited meant staying out. in front, so I couldn't be forgotten. Staying ahead meant staying in control. Stillness, by contrast, had been associated with risk—missed details, dropped balls, consequences I'd have to clean up later.

So when life finally slowed, my nervous system didn't recognize it as safety.

It recognized it as danger.

This is what happens when survival becomes a lifestyle.

I didn't live in crisis every day, but I lived prepared for one. I anticipated needs before they surfaced. I stayed mentally ahead of conversations, schedules, outcomes. I carried contingency plans without realizing it. Even moments that looked calm on the outside were often filled with internal vigilance.

When that vigilance no longer had somewhere to go, it turned inward.

I noticed how quickly I filled quiet moments.

If the house was still, I reached for my phone.

If my mind was quiet, I replayed conversations.

If nothing needed solving, I invented problems to prepare for.

Marketable

Stillness wasn't neutral.

It triggered a sense of vulnerability I didn't yet know how to sit with.

Rest asked something of me I hadn't practiced before: trust.

Scripture names this connection directly:

"Trust in the Lord with all your heart."

—Proverbs 3:5-6

Quietness and trust are not automatic states. They are learned. They develop through repetition, not intention alone. And the more you practice handing it over to God, the more you stop trying to carry what was never yours to control, and the quieter your mind becomes. The lighter your heart feels. The more naturally peace begins to return.

Miss Clara in the movie War Room became a reminder for me. Not because she made prayer feel dramatic—but because she made it practical. She didn't treat prayer like an accessory you add after you've exhausted yourself. She treated it like a strategy. A way of stepping out of the driver's seat and letting God do what only God can do. Sometimes the most spiritual thing you can do is stop rehearsing the problem, stop replaying the disrespect, stop fueling the fear—and take it to the closet. Not to perform. To be repositioned. And to let God do the fighting for me.

I had to relearn what safety felt like without urgency attached to it.

That process wasn't intellectual. It was physical.

I noticed it in my breathing first. Shallow at rest. I noticed it in my shoulders—still lifted even when nothing was required of me. I noticed it in how quickly my thoughts raced when there was nothing demanding them.

My body hadn't caught up to my circumstances yet.

So I didn't force rest to feel good.

I practiced staying.

I allowed myself to sit in stillness without correcting it. Without explaining it. Without filling it. I reminded myself—sometimes out loud—that nothing was wrong simply because nothing was happening.

Rest wasn't a signal that I was falling behind.

It was evidence that I had stopped running.

That distinction mattered.

As I stayed with the discomfort, rest began to surface beliefs I hadn't questioned before.

If I'm not producing, am I still valuable?

If I'm not responding immediately, will I be forgotten?

If I'm not managing everything, will something fall apart?

Those questions weren't new.

They had just been drowned out by activity.

Stillness didn't create fear.

It revealed it.

Scripture offered grounding again:

"Be still, and know that I am God."

—Psalm 46:10

That verse isn't a suggestion to relax. It's a reorientation of authority. It reminds us that the world does not rest on our vigilance.

Rest asked me to surrender control in small, unglamorous ways.

To let emails wait.

To allow someone else to handle something imperfectly.

To trust that silence didn't mean abandonment or punishment.

This was especially hard because silence had once felt dangerous to me. Quiet used to mean something was wrong—or about to be. I had learned to fill space quickly, to smooth tension before it could grow.

Now, I was learning that silence could also mean peace.

That it didn't always need to be managed.

As my nervous system slowly recalibrated, I noticed changes I hadn't expected. I slept deeper. My body softened. My thoughts slowed without effort. The constant low-level tension I had normalized began to loosen its grip.

Rest stopped feeling like something I had to earn.

It started feeling like something I was allowed.

That shift didn't happen all at once. Some days, stillness felt grounding. Other days, it felt unsettling again. But each time I returned to it, the fear lost a little authority.

I trusted myself more.

I trusted that I could pause without everything unraveling. That I could be present without being hyper-vigilant. That I didn't need to stay alert to stay safe.

Rest didn't make me weaker.

It made me regulated.

And regulation changed how I showed up everywhere else. I was less reactive. Less defensive. Less anticipatory. I responded instead of bracing. I listened instead of scanning.

Once safety returned to stillness, rest became something I returned to—not something I avoided.

Marketable

It became a place of grounding rather than exposure.

And perhaps most importantly, rest reminded me of something I had forgotten in years of motion:

I am not held together by effort alone.

I am allowed to stop.

You are never starting from zero again.

Hold This

Rest can feel unsafe when your body has been trained to survive. That doesn't mean you're failing. It means your nervous system is still learning what your faith already knows: you are held, even when you're still.

Try This

Practice a 3-Minute Rest Rewire once a day for seven days:

- Name what's happening (10 seconds):

"My body is bracing. Nothing is wrong. This is conditioning."

- Breathe low and slow (90 seconds):
- Inhale for 4, exhale for 6.
- Put one hand on your chest and one on your stomach.

Release one responsibility (30 seconds):

- Say: "God, this is Yours. I'm not carrying it right now."

Do one "still" action (30 seconds):

- Sit. Stand outside. Wash one dish slowly. Walk to the mailbox without your phone.

Let your body experience: nothing is happening—and I am safe.

If your mind starts inventing problems, gently return to one sentence:

"Stillness isn't danger. It's restoration."

Chapter 18
Relearning Joy After Survival

"Strong was my brand. Peace became my choice."
— Brittany P. Webb

At first, joy felt suspicious.

Not because I didn't want it—but because my nervous system had been trained to brace for the next thing.

Even peace had edges. Even quiet felt like a setup.

Relearning joy was less like a party and more like therapy: slow, awkward at times, and often found in small moments I used to rush past. I noticed it. I appreciated it. I even welcomed it. But I was afraid to truly embrace it, because history had taught me how quickly good things could be taken away. The other shoe would drop—and it was a long way back.

That's how it felt for me.

I had done the work to slow down. I had learned how to rest. I had stopped living in constant anticipation. And still, joy didn't come rushing back like a fireworks show. It came like light under a door—quiet, steady, almost shy. There was a neutral space first: a calm without sparkle... and then glimpses of shimmer.

And for a while, that calm felt hopeful—but flat.

I wondered if something was wrong with me.

I wasn't sad. I wasn't anxious. But I wasn't bubbling over either. The adrenaline that once fueled me was gone, and in its place was a quieter nervous system that didn't know how to celebrate yet.

This is something we don't talk about enough.

Survival gives you intensity.

Healing gives you neutrality first.

Joy has to be relearned.

In survival mode, joy is often loud or urgent. It shows up as relief. As distraction. As escape. It has sharp edges because it's competing with pain.

But after survival, joy becomes subtle, sometimes hand in hand with gratitude.

Marketable

It shows up in moments you might have once overlooked: a slow morning. A deep breath that reaches the bottom of your lungs. Laughter that isn't covering anything, or catches you by surprise. A sense of being content without needing to prove it. A cool breeze moving through your hair on a hot, sunny day.

At first, I didn't recognize those moments as joy.

They felt too small.

I had been conditioned to expect joy to arrive as a reward for endurance. Something earned after pushing through. Something dramatic enough to justify the cost of everything I had carried.

But joy after survival doesn't arrive with fireworks.

It arrives with permission.

Permission to enjoy something without explaining why. Permission to like something without turning it into a goal. Permission to feel good without bracing for the drop.

That took practice.

I had to notice joy when it appeared—without dismissing it. Without saying this won't last. Without immediately asking what's next?

Those habits were deeply ingrained.

I had trained myself to move quickly from moment to moment, always scanning forward. Joy requires presence. Survival does not.

Scripture reflects this shift gently:

"The joy of the Lord is your strength."

—Nehemiah 8:10

Joy isn't the result of strength.

It is the source of it.

That reframed everything for me. I used to think I had to get strong first—then joy would follow. But joy was part of the training. The more I practiced it, the more it became muscle memory, and the longer it stayed.

I began to notice joy in ordinary places.

In conversations that didn't revolve around problem-solving.

In creativity that wasn't monetized or measured.

In choosing rest without guilt.

In my home.

In the grocery store.

Joy wasn't loud.

It was steady.

And because it was steady, it felt vulnerable.

I noticed how quickly I wanted to minimize it. To stay neutral instead of hopeful. To avoid disappointment by keeping expectations low. Survival teaches you not to hope too much Disappointment often shows up when we turn hope becomes an expectation, and expectation becomes demand.

But healing asks something different.

It asks you to risk enjoyment.

Joy after survival doesn't demand constant happiness. It doesn't ignore grief or minimize pain. It exists alongside realism. It knows that life still holds uncertainty—but it refuses to let uncertainty dictate the present.

That balance was new for me.

I learned that joy doesn't require me to be naïve. It requires me to be present. To let good moments be good without immediately analyzing their shelf life.

This also meant letting joy look different than it used to.

It wasn't productivity-driven.

It wasn't fueled by validation.

It wasn't tied to achievement.

It was quieter. More internal. Less performative.

Joy didn't mean my life was perfect.

It meant my life was mine.

Scripture names this simplicity beautifully:

"A cheerful heart is good medicine."

—Proverbs 17:22

Joy healed parts of me that productivity never touched. It softened my edges. It restored curiosity. It made space for creativity without pressure.

And slowly, joy began to expand and stay around longer.

Not because I chased it—but because I allowed it.

I stopped asking joy to prove itself. I let it come and go without judgment. I trusted that if it left for a moment, it would return again.

That trust was new.

Joy no longer felt fragile. It felt resilient. And steady.

I didn't need joy to be constant. I needed it to be honest.

And honest joy doesn't shout.

It settles.

It blesses.

It refreshes the soul.

It reminds you that survival was not the end of the story.

It was the beginning of something gentler—and no less powerful.

Marketable

You are never starting from zero again. You're starting from experience.

Hold This

Joy doesn't have to be loud to be real. Sometimes the strongest joy is the quiet kind—the kind that returns when your nervous system finally believes it's safe.

Try This

For the next seven days, practice Joy Without Demand:
- Each morning, write one sentence: "Today, joy can look like ____."

(Keep it small: a slow coffee, a walk, a clean kitchen, a deep breath, a song.)
- Each evening, write two lines:
  - "I noticed joy when ____."
  - "I didn't rush past it—I stayed for ____ seconds."

If disappointment tries to hijack the day, repeat this reframe:

"Hope is allowed here. Demand is not."

The goal isn't to force happiness. It's to train your mind and body to recognize peace—and let joy stay a little longer.

Chapter 19
Motherhood After Overfunctioning

"I thought I was selling my skills. I was really selling my peace."
— Brittany P. Webb

I didn't realize how much of my motherhood had been built on overfunctioning until I stopped.

From the outside, I looked like a capable, present, involved mother. And I was. I loved my children deeply. I showed up. I handled logistics. I anticipated needs before they were spoken. I filled gaps quickly and quietly.

But underneath that competence was a constant hum of responsibility.

I held everything in my head.

Schedules. Deadlines. Emotional shifts. School projects. Forgotten forms. Dinner plans. Every dang day. Future worries. The invisible work of anticipating what might be needed next—by any one of them, at any time.

I thought that was what good mothers did.

I thought being prepared was the same as being present.

But over time, I realized something uncomfortable: I wasn't just supporting my children—I was buffering them from discomfort at the cost of my own nervous system.

I fixed things before they felt the weight of them.

I jumped in before they struggled.

I absorbed stress so they didn't have to.

Even admitting that, I can hear the little voice in me defending it: That's what mother's do. We love our kids. and We don't want them to carry what feels heavy.

That felt loving.

It was also exhausting.

When I began setting boundaries and practicing rest, motherhood was one of the hardest places to let go. Not because my children demanded everything—but because I had trained myself to be everything.

I had to face the truth that my overfunctioning didn't just protect them.

It limited them.

When I stopped managing every detail, something shifted. At first, it was uncomfortable—for all of us. Things were forgotten. Homework wasn't always perfect. Emotions surfaced without immediate solutions.

Marketable

And I wanted to step back in.

That urge was strong.

But I resisted it—not because I stopped caring, but because I cared enough to let them grow.

Motherhood after overfunctioning required me to tolerate discomfort. To let my children experience frustration without rescuing them. To allow them to solve problems imperfectly. To trust that struggle didn't mean failure.

That was hard.

It required me to sit on my hands sometimes—emotionally and literally. To pause before fixing. To ask, Is this mine to carry—or theirs to learn?

Scripture reminds us:

"Each one should carry their own load."

—Galatians 6:5

That verse doesn't negate support. It clarifies responsibility.

Letting my children carry age-appropriate weight wasn't abandonment. It was respect.

I noticed how the atmosphere of our home began to change.

There was more honesty.

More shared responsibility.

More respect for the weight of tasks.

More room for real conversation instead of constant management.

I became less reactive. Less rushed. Less depleted.

And surprisingly, my children rose.

They became more capable. More expressive. More willing to try. More willing to own their chores. And over time, I noticed more gratitude—not just from them, but in me.

When I stopped filling every space, they stepped into it. And they did it with grace, out of love.

Motherhood became less about control and more about connection.

That shift didn't mean I stopped being involved. It meant I stopped being consumed.

I was no longer parenting from a place of vigilance. I was parenting from presence.

When my kids were younger, so much of motherhood was teaching, protecting, fixing, caretaking, anticipating, and nurturing. It was hands-on in a way that left little room for anything else—because "keeping them alive" really was the job. And raising them in the way of the Lord.

But as they've gotten older, presence has mattered in a different way—maybe even more. There's so much a parent can't control once children grow into teens and young adults. You can't manage every outcome. You can't protect them from every consequence. You can't always fix what they feel.

What you can offer is steady presence. Clear availability. Consistent guidance. A home they can return to—emotionally and spiritually—even when life gets complicated.

And that's when I started noticing how much modeling mattered.

When my children saw me rest without guilt, they learned rest wasn't something to earn.

When they saw me say "no" calmly, they learned boundaries weren't cruelty.

When they saw me regulate instead of react, they learned emotional steadiness without a lecture.

That kind of teaching doesn't come from instruction.

It comes from embodiment.

Motherhood after overfunctioning is quieter.

Not because it lacks love—but because love no longer needs to prove itself through exhaustion. The house doesn't run on urgency anymore. It runs on rhythm.

That rhythm isn't perfect.

But it's not insanity, either.

It's a slower-paced, *if you're here, be here* kind of vibe.

I believe good mothers take shape in all different ways. And I respect each good mother out there. But for me, and for our home, I no longer believe I'll somehow lose my "good mother" award if I don't foresee and address every little thing. Instead, I believe that I can stay present inside myself and my home while raising strong, capable, and kind humans who can do the same.

Overfunctioning once felt like devotion.

Now, it feels like distrust.

Trust—in myself, in my children, and in the process—changed everything.

Motherhood didn't become easier.

It became truer.

You are never starting from zero again. You're starting from experience.

Marketable

Hold This

Being a good mother is not the same thing as being the family's nervous system. Your love doesn't have to sound like urgency to be real.

Try This

Practice "Step Back Without Stepping Away" for seven days:

1.   Pick one area you normally over-manage (homework reminders, laundry, rides, chores, school emails, last-minute saves).

2.   Choose one small shift: don't rescue first. Pause first.

Use this line (out loud or in your head):

"I'm going to let them feel the weight—age-appropriate weight—so they can grow strong."

If they struggle, try one of these responses instead of taking over:
- "What do you think your next step is?"
- "I believe you can handle this. I'm here if you want help thinking it through."
- "I'm not going to fix it for you, but I'll sit with you while you figure it out."

End the day with one sentence:

"Today, I parented from presence instead of vigilance."

Chapter 20
Building From Alignment, Not Approval

"The asset wasn't the project. It was me."
— Brittany P. Webb

Once I understood what the asset actually was, everything changed.

Not all at once.

Not dramatically.

But decisively.

Before, creation had always been tied to approval. I built within systems. I shaped myself to environments. I waited for signals — encouragement, permission, consensus — before trusting my instincts.

That wasn't weakness.

It was conditioning.

When you are competent and dependable, you learn quickly what is rewarded. You learn how to read rooms. You learn how to anticipate expectations. You learn how to succeed inside structures that already exist.

What you don't always learn is how to build without reference points.

That kind of creation requires something different.

It requires self-trust.

When Approval Is No Longer the Starting Point

After the internal shift, I noticed something subtle but profound.

I stopped asking, Will this work?

And started asking, Does this fit?

Fit became more important than feasibility. Alignment mattered more than optics. I no longer felt compelled to explain my ideas before they were fully formed or to soften them so they would be easier for others to receive.

I didn't need to convince.

I needed to listen — inwardly.

This was unfamiliar territory. When you've spent years building inside systems, the absence of structure can feel like instability. But what I discovered was that alignment creates its own structure.

It just doesn't announce itself.

Why Starting Over Didn't Feel Like Failure

From the outside, it might have looked like I was starting over.

New direction.

119

Marketable

New systems.

New ideas.

But internally, it didn't register that way at all.

Starting over implies loss — of progress, of credibility, of momentum.

What I felt instead was coherence.

Nothing I had lived, learned, or built was wasted. It had simply been recontextualized. The skills remained. The insight remained. The capacity remained.

What was gone was the pressure to optimize myself for environments that required overextension.

I wasn't rebuilding from scratch.

I was rebuilding from truth.

That distinction matters.

When you build from truth, you don't rush. You don't panic. You don't need immediate validation to keep going. You allow ideas to mature before exposing them to the world.

You trust your timing.

Creation Without Self-Erasure

This was the first time I built something without disappearing inside it.

I didn't abandon my values to meet expectations.

I didn't sacrifice peace to maintain momentum.

I didn't confuse urgency with importance.

Instead, I asked different questions:

Does this honor the life I'm living now?

Does this require me to override my body or intuition?

Does this align with the person I am becoming?

If the answer was no, I let it go.

That was new.

Before, I would have tried to make it work anyway — reshaping myself to fit the demand. But now, the asset I was protecting was not the project.

It was me.

And protecting that asset changed the quality of everything I built.

The Freedom to Choose What Not to Build

One of the greatest benefits of reclaiming self-trust was this:

I no longer felt obligated to build everything I was capable of building.

Just because I could do something didn't mean I should.

That freedom is rarely talked about — especially for high-capacity women. We are praised for versatility, adaptability, and resilience. We are encouraged to stretch, to take on more, to prove range.

But range without restraint becomes depletion.

Once I understood my value wasn't tied to output, I could finally say no without fear. I didn't need to justify my choices. I didn't need to monetize every idea or pursue every opportunity.

Discernment became the metric.

Why the Asset Changes Everything

A woman who knows she is the asset builds differently.

She doesn't chase relevance.

She doesn't fear pauses.

She doesn't overexplain.

She doesn't abandon herself to stay visible.

She knows that what she brings to any table is not just skill — it is presence, clarity, and steadiness.

Those qualities don't disappear with change.

They deepen.

And because of that, she is free to create — or rest — without losing her sense of worth.

That freedom is what makes rebuilding possible without fear.

Not because the outcome is guaranteed.

But because she is.

What This Means Going Forward

Marketable is not a promise that everything will work out neatly.

It's a promise that you will not lose yourself in the process.

That you can begin again without erasing what came before.

That you can build without betraying your body, your values, or your faith.

That you can choose alignment over approval and still create something meaningful.

The greatest shift was not what I built next.

It was how I stood while building.

Grounded.

Regulated.

Whole.

And that posture — more than any credential or title — is what makes a woman marketable in every season of life.

Marketable

And the me I recovered is the most marketable asset I've ever owned.

I recovered myself.

At some point along the way, what I had prayed for years before showed up in a form I didn't predict: visibility without begging for it. Proof without pleading for it. A quiet kind of credibility that didn't require me to relive my worst chapter to earn trust in my next one.

I even rebuilt the way I showed up in the world—website, messaging, merchandise, the whole ecosystem—because for the first time, my external brand matched my internal becoming.

I poured what I was learning into books. I developed Prompt Therapy™ as a real, usable practice—not a performance, not a trend, but a way to meet yourself with truth and let God meet you there too. I shaped B Creative Systems and the frameworks that now carry my work—12.5 Signature Marketing System™, B10 Core Automation™, and Bline™, a backend system being built to help others run their businesses with clarity instead of chaos.

And here's the part that still humbles me: the fruit didn't come from striving harder. It came from becoming more honest.

One makes you frantic for feedback. The other makes you faithful with your next step.

Alignment makes you plant.

Approval makes you chase.

That's the difference between building from approval and building from alignment.

I built because I finally believed I was valuable—before any result could validate it.

I didn't build to prove I was valuable.

I wrote. I built. I learned how to sit with my own thoughts long enough to separate what was true from what was loud. I turned my reflection into language, my language into frameworks, and my frameworks into a new kind of work—work that wasn't dependent on anyone's permission.

And in the quiet, something unexpected grew.

That shift didn't happen in one brave moment. It happened in a hundred small ones—when I chose integrity over retaliation, quiet over commentary, and obedience over the urge to manage how I was perceived.

I stopped asking, "Do you see me?" and started asking, "God, what do You see?"

So I stopped auditioning.

There was a season when I was legally boxed in—quieted by paperwork, restrictions, and the lingering ache of a chapter I wasn't allowed to explain. I wasn't free to "tell my side," and truthfully, I wasn't sure I even wanted to. I just knew I couldn't keep trying to prove my worth to a system that had already decided what it needed to believe to protect itself.

It cost me approval first.

Alignment sounds like a clean word until it starts costing you approval. *You are never starting from zero again. You're starting from experience.*

Hold This

Alignment can feel like loss at first—loss of approval, loss of familiarity, loss of who people thought you were. But what you lose in approval, you gain in authority: the quiet authority of becoming who God is forming you to be.

Try This

- Write two columns: Approval (what you do to be liked) and Alignment (what you do to be faithful to yourself).
- Circle one Approval habit you're ready to release this week.
- Choose one Alignment action you can take in the next 24 hours—small, specific, and doable.
- Pray: "God, help me obey without auditioning."

If you feel fear after you choose alignment, don't interpret that as a sign you did it wrong. Fear is often just the old system noticing you changed.

Chapter 21
When Shared Systems Change

"When I changed, the rhythm changed—without anyone being the villain."
— Brittany P. Webb

When one person changes, the system around them has to respond.

Not immediately.

Not always willingly.

But inevitably.

For a long time, I believed that if I changed quietly enough, nothing else would need to adjust. That I could grow internally while keeping external systems intact. That I could do my work privately and spare everyone else the discomfort of recalibration.

That belief was kind.

It was also unrealistic.

Every system—family, work, partnership, friendship—has a rhythm. An unspoken agreement about who carries what, who initiates, who absorbs, who steadies. When one person stops overfunctioning, the system notices.

Even if no one names it.

At first, I tried to make my changes invisible. I set boundaries softly. I paused instead of reacted. I reduced my emotional output without announcing why. I told myself that if I didn't make a big deal out of it, nothing would be disrupted.

But systems don't respond to words.

They respond to patterns.

When my patterns changed, the system had to reorganize.

That reorganization wasn't dramatic. It didn't involve ultimatums or confrontations. It showed up in subtler ways—moments of uncertainty, pauses where someone else waited for me to step in, silences where I used to fill the space.

And for a while, that space felt uncomfortable.

Not because something was wrong, but because something was different.

I had been the emotional stabilizer in many of my shared systems. The one who anticipated tension and smoothed it before it surfaced. The one who carried unspoken responsibility so things could keep moving without friction.

When I stopped doing that, the system lost its shock absorber.

That wasn't cruelty.

It was honesty.

I had to learn to tolerate the discomfort of letting others feel what I used to absorb. To allow moments to unfold without rushing to manage them. To trust that silence didn't mean disconnection and that tension didn't require immediate repair.

This was especially true in the most intimate systems of my life.

When one person wakes up—really wakes up—the system often resists before it adapts. Not out of malice, but out of habit. Familiar dynamics feel safe, even when they're no longer healthy.

I learned that growth doesn't ask permission.

It invites participation.

Scripture reflects this principle without naming roles or outcomes:

"Do not conform to the pattern of this world, but be transformed by the renewing of your mind."

—Romans 12:2

Transformation is internal first. External systems catch up later.

I had to accept that not everyone would immediately understand my changes. Some would misinterpret them. Some would assume distance where there was simply differentiation. Some would need time to find their footing in the new rhythm.

And I had to resist the urge to explain myself back into old patterns.

That restraint was hard.

My instinct was to soothe. To clarify. To reassure. To step back into the role that made everyone comfortable again—even if it cost me.

But growth asked me to stay put.

To trust that systems can stretch without breaking.

To allow others to step forward where I stepped back.

To believe that shared responsibility creates stronger bonds than silent sacrifice ever did.

Over time, something unexpected happened.

The systems adjusted.

Not all at once. Not without friction. But slowly, new rhythms emerged. Responsibilities redistributed. Conversations changed tone. Expectations recalibrated.

Marketable

I didn't disappear.

I differentiated.

That distinction mattered.

Differentiation isn't withdrawal. It's clarity. It allows connection without fusion. Partnership without overfunctioning. Presence without performance.

I learned that healthy systems don't rely on one person carrying emotional weight for everyone else. They require participation. Accountability. Mutual awareness.

When I stopped holding everything together, I discovered that togetherness didn't disappear.

It matured.

This chapter isn't about conflict or resolution. It's about rebalancing. About trusting that shared systems can survive growth—even when it feels destabilizing at first.

Because what feels like loss is often just transition.

What feels like distance is often just space.

And what feels like disruption may be the very thing that allows a system to become more honest, more resilient, and more real.

I didn't need to tear anything down.

I needed to stop propping things up alone.

And once I did, I learned something important:

Shared systems don't break when one person wakes up.

They evolve.

It means more sustainable.

And shared doesn't mean less loving.

But space is where shared systems become shared.

That space may feel like discomfort at first—especially if you were praised for being "the strong one."

That's the part I wish more women were told earlier: when you stop filling every gap, you create space for capability to develop.

And the people who were ready to grow with me… rose.

It didn't always go perfectly. But it went better than my fear predicted.

I let my children feel the weight of age-appropriate tasks. I let my team members solve problems without me rescuing the outcome. I let relationships carry silence without me filling it.

I also learned to do something that felt almost wrong at first: I started giving other people the dignity of responsibility.

Because every time you sprint to fix someone else's feelings, you're teaching the system that your boundaries are negotiable.

Let them choose distance if your growth makes them uncomfortable.

Let them misunderstand you.

Let them be disappointed.

Mel Robbins has a phrase that helped me detach from overmanaging other people's reactions: "Let them."

And instead of chasing them, I practiced the simplest, hardest discipline: letting the system reveal itself.

I learned to expect a little resistance without taking it personally. Some people adjusted. Some didn't. Some tried to guilt me back into my old role. Some quietly moved away when my new boundaries didn't serve their needs.

And "new" is threatening to people who benefited from the old version of you.

Sometimes it means you're new.

Pushback doesn't always mean you're wrong.

This is where pushback can mess with your head if you don't name it.

So when I changed, it created friction—not because I suddenly became selfish, but because the old system depended on my overgiving to stay comfortable.

That's what systems do: they adapt around what's consistent. And for years, my consistency had been availability.

I had been the overfunctioner for so long that my first boundary felt, to other people, like abandonment.

I had been the fixer for so long that my first pause looked like neglect.

I had been the "yes" girl for so long that my first "not right now" sounded like rebellion.

When I started resetting my patterns—at home, at work, and inside myself—the whole system felt it. Not because the change was wrong, but because it disrupted what everyone had learned to expect.

Shared systems are beautiful until one person decides to change the rules. *You are never starting from zero again. You're starting from experience.*

Hold This

Marketable

When you change, the system will resist. That resistance is not proof you're selfish—it's proof the system depended on you overfunctioning to stay comfortable.

Try This

- Name one area where you overfunction (home, work, friendship, family).
- Write the new expectation in one sentence (example: "I will not fix it before they feel it.").
- Decide what you will do instead of rescuing (pause, delegate, wait 24 hours, ask a question).
- Practice "Let them" once today—then come back to your own peace.
  Shared systems take time to recalibrate. Give the new rhythm space to settle.

Chapter 22
Faith Without Performance

"God doesn't need me polished. He wants my presence."
— Brittany P. Webb

For a long time, I treated faith like another role to execute well.

Say the right things.

Hold it together.

Be encouraging.

Be "fine."

But faith—real faith—doesn't require a polished version of you. It asks for the honest one.

And that honesty is where my spiritual life stopped feeling like performance and started feeling like home.

For most of my life, faith was something I practiced well.

I showed up.

I served.

I believed the right things.

From the outside, my faith looked steady and intact. And in many ways, it was sincere. I loved God deeply. I trusted Him. I leaned on Scripture. I prayed often.

But beneath that devotion lived an unspoken equation:

Faith + effort = security.

I didn't articulate it that way, but I lived it. I believed that if I stayed faithful enough, disciplined enough, obedient enough, things would hold together. That my responsibility was to do my part fully so God could do His.

But looking back, I can admit something I didn't know how to name at the time:

I believed faith was supposed to make me feel secure.

And in 2017, God disrupted that belief in a way I still can't fully explain.

We were on a trip. Zac Brown Band. A fun night. Late-night pizza back at the hotel—one of my favorite little traditions. I fell asleep grateful.

Marketable

Then sometime in the night, I woke up and stood… and my body gave out. I went down hard—hit the corner of the wall. And in the split second between floor and fear, the room did something strange. I saw bright yellow light. And I heard a calm voice—so steady it almost felt like peace with words.

This wasn't a desire to escape life. I believe light will overcome darkness, and the sun will come up tomorrow. I believe this was mercy—a wake-up, a reminder of how loving and powerful and quick our lives here can be, and an invitation to choose it fully—to fight for my family and all the things I hadn't done yet and didn't yet know I'd need to.

What I heard wasn't a detailed instruction—it was simple, and it landed with startling clarity:
"You can let it all go; I've got you. Or choose to stay—but you're going to have to fight."
As fast as I could fathom the speed of light might be, I chose to fight. I woke up and life returned to normal. But I couldn't forget that event, until I did, and it was sooner that I'd like to admit.

That night should've changed everything. In some ways, it did.
But I truly didn't have the foresight to understand what that fight He referenced would come to mean.

In fact, for years, I barely remembered that life-changing moment while I was drowning in performance culture and the darkness that came with it.
It wasn't until the quiet, the peace, the reflections, and the healing were evident—eight years later—and it hit me like a ton of bricks. He reminded me, and the flood gates opened as tears rolled town my face. I understood. The last eight years flashed before my eyes, lots of memories, good and hard, and finally understood what He meant by fight. I found my way back to His light in the strongest, biggest way

Over time, my faith had become intertwined with performance.
Not in a loud or legalistic way — but in a subtle, exhausting one. I prayed, but I also pushed. I trusted, but I also managed. I surrendered, but I kept one hand firmly on the wheel.
I didn't realize how much effort I was expending to be a "good" believer.

When my life slowed down — when productivity loosened its grip and survival mode ended — something unexpected happened to my faith.

It got quieter.

At first, that quiet made me uneasy.

I was used to faith being active, verbal, demonstrative. Used to doing something with it. Used to processing, explaining, asking, seeking reassurance.

Now, there was space.

And in that space, I had to face a question I had avoided for years:

Who am I in my faith when I'm not striving?

That question wasn't theoretical.

It surfaced in ordinary moments — sitting alone without urgency, praying without an agenda, reading Scripture without looking for instruction or confirmation. Faith was no longer something I used to stabilize my effort.

It was something I rested into.

That shift was uncomfortable.

Without performance, I had to trust that God wasn't measuring me by output. That I didn't need to prove my devotion through exhaustion. That belief didn't require constant demonstration.

Scripture had always said this.

I had just skimmed past it.

"Be still, and know that I am God."

—Psalm 46:10

Stillness isn't passive.

It's relational.

In stillness, I couldn't hide behind service or competence. I couldn't substitute activity for intimacy. I had to sit with God as I was — not as who I thought I needed to be.

That exposure was tender.

I noticed how often my prayers had been shaped by responsibility. I prayed for outcomes. For protection. For wisdom to manage what I was carrying. I prayed as someone accountable for holding everything together.

Now, my prayers changed tone.

They became simpler.

Sometimes they were wordless.

Sometimes they were gratitude.

Sometimes they were just presence.

I didn't need faith to motivate me anymore.

Marketable

I needed faith to hold me.

That reorientation revealed how much pressure I had placed on myself spiritually. I had conflated faithfulness with endurance. Belief with resilience. Trust with effort.

But faith without performance asked something different.

It asked me to receive.

To believe that God was present even when I wasn't productive. That He didn't require my anxiety to stay involved in my life. That I could rest without falling behind spiritually.

"My grace is sufficient for you, for my power is made perfect in weakness."

—2 Corinthians 12:9

Weakness wasn't something to overcome anymore.

It was something to allow.

Faith became less about proving my devotion and more about trusting His presence. Less about getting it right and more about staying open. Less about certainty and more about relationship.

That shift softened me.

I stopped performing strength in prayer. I stopped editing my honesty. I allowed doubt to exist without panicking. I allowed peace to coexist with unanswered questions.

Faith didn't become smaller.

It became truer.

I also noticed how faith without performance affected how I treated others. I became less judgmental — of myself and of them. Less attached to appearances. Less concerned with how belief looked and more attentive to how it felt.

I no longer needed faith to justify my choices.

I trusted it to guide them.

Faith without performance didn't make me passive.

It made me grounded.

It allowed me to act from alignment instead of fear. To trust God's timing instead of forcing outcomes. To believe that obedience doesn't always look impressive — sometimes it looks like restraint.

Sometimes it looks like rest.

Sometimes it looks like saying no.

Sometimes it looks like doing less and trusting more.

I didn't lose my faith when I stopped striving.

I found it.

Stripped of performance.

Freed from pressure.

Rooted in presence.

And once faith no longer required me to hold everything together, I realized something profound:

I never had to.

Not because my life suddenly got easier, but because I stopped trying to earn what God had already given.

Relief.

And once I let my faith become relational again—not transactional—I started to feel something I hadn't felt in a long time:

He heals the one who tells the truth.

Because God can't heal the version of you that's pretending.

That's where healing accelerates.

You start bringing the real things to God—not the curated things.

You stop apologizing for having needs.

You stop repenting for being human.

Faith without performance also changes how you repent.

And asking for help is not a spiritual flaw.

Silence is not weakness.

Boundaries are not rebellion.

And if that's true, then rest is not laziness.

But being made in God's image means your worth is not a reward for good performance. It is a starting point.

Until we're not the strong one anymore.

Until we don't meet the standard.

Until we disappoint someone.

Because somewhere along the way, many of us start acting like we're loved by God—until we fail.

That verse is familiar, but living like it is a whole different thing.

"By grace you have been saved through faith... not by works." — Ephesians 2:8–9

Scripture makes it painfully clear that grace isn't a reward for effort:

And for me, it looked like letting the "good girl" in me retire.

It looks like trusting God's character more than your own consistency.

It looks like worshiping while your life still feels unresolved.

It looks like praying before you have the right words.

Marketable

Not polished. Not packaged. Honest.

Faith without performance looks like this: showing up honest.

But the longer I lived like that, the more exhausted my soul became.

I don't think I meant to build that theology. I think I absorbed it—from culture, from leadership, from the way people reward strength and avoid discomfort.

The kind where you feel closer to Him when you're "handling it well," and farther when you're messy, unsure, or emotional.

The kind where you believe God is pleased with you when you're productive, and disappointed when you're tired.

The subtler kind.

Not the kind of performance that's obvious—like standing on a stage or checking boxes to look holy.

I didn't realize how much of my faith had quietly merged with performance until I stopped performing.

You are never starting from zero again. You're starting from experience.

Hold This

God is not measuring your worth by your output. Grace is not a reward for being "good." It's a gift that meets you as you are and strengthens you as you grow.

Try This

- Finish this sentence honestly: "I feel most lovable when I'm _____."
- Ask yourself: "Is that belief from God… or from a performance-based environment?"
- Pick one "work" you've been using to earn peace (overexplaining, overgiving, overdoing) and release it for one day.
- Read Ephesians 2:8–9 slowly and write what it means in your own words. Faith becomes lighter when you stop performing and start relating.

Chapter 23
Healing the Body That Held Everything

"My body was the first place the truth showed up."
— Brittany P. Webb

My healing was not only emotional. It was physical. My body had been keeping score for years—through stress flareups, through anxious spirals, through the kind of "I'm fine" that convinced everyone except my nervous system. There were seasons I medicated the symptoms, and seasons I numbed the feelings.

At my lowest, even a nightly bottle of wine didn't feel like indulgence—it felt like sedation.

And then, slowly, I chose a different kind of relief: sleep, water, prayer, movement, and the hard honesty of actually feeling what I'd been avoiding. Over time—through boundaries, support, and healthier rhythms—I lost weight, regained strength, and (with medical guidance) no longer needed what I once depended on just to get through the day.

My body knew long before I was willing to listen.

It knew in the tension I carried in my shoulders, always lifted, always braced.

It knew in the shallow breaths I took without noticing.

It knew in the exhaustion that sleep didn't touch and the alertness that never fully shut off.

For years, my body adapted to what my life required of it. It stayed ready. It stayed responsive. It stayed strong.

It held everything.

I didn't think of my body as something that needed care beyond basic maintenance. It was a vehicle — one that needed to function reliably so I could keep going. I trusted it to keep up, and it did.

Until it couldn't.

What I've learned since is this: the body doesn't rebel. It communicates.

Mine communicated through fatigue. Through tension. Through symptoms that came and went depending on how much stress I was carrying. Through signals I minimized because they were inconvenient or didn't fit the pace of my life.

Marketable

I told myself I was fine.

My body disagreed.

Healing didn't begin when I decided to "take better care of myself." It began when I stopped treating my body like a machine and started recognizing it as a partner — one that had been compensating for me for a long time.

The first shift was awareness.

I noticed how often I ignored physical cues. Hunger. Thirst. The need to stretch. The need to rest. I had trained myself to override discomfort because there was always something more important to do.

That override became habit.

And habits leave marks.

When I slowed down, my body didn't immediately relax. Like my nervous system, it had learned vigilance. It stayed tight even in safety. It held tension even when there was no demand.

Healing wasn't instant relief.

It was reacquaintance.

I had to learn what rest felt like in my body — not as collapse, but as regulation. I had to relearn how to breathe fully, how to sit without bracing, how to notice sensations without judging them.

I discovered how much emotion lives in the body.

Grief didn't just exist in my thoughts. It lived in my chest.

Anxiety wasn't just worry. It was tightness, shallow breath, a racing pulse.

Relief wasn't just mental. It was warmth, softness, ease.

Once I started listening, I realized my body had been telling the truth all along.

Scripture speaks to this more than we often acknowledge:

"Do you not know that your bodies are temples of the Holy Spirit?"

—1 Corinthians 6:19

A temple isn't something you push through.

It's something you tend.

Healing the body required gentleness — something I wasn't practiced in. I knew how to push. I knew how to endure. Gentleness felt foreign, even indulgent.

But gentleness turned out to be necessary.

I stopped forcing workouts that punished instead of nourished.

I prioritized sleep without treating it as negotiable.

I noticed how food affected my energy and mood rather than following rules.

I allowed my body to recover without rushing it toward productivity.

These changes weren't dramatic.

They were respectful.

And respect, I learned, was what my body had been missing.

As my body healed, my relationship with it changed. I stopped seeing physical limits as weaknesses. I stopped interpreting fatigue as failure. I understood that rest wasn't laziness — it was repair.

There were days when emotions surfaced unexpectedly through physical sensation. Tightness would release, and tears would follow. Relaxation would arrive, and exhaustion would show itself.

That wasn't regression.

That was processing.

My body had been holding stories my mind hadn't fully acknowledged yet.

Healing didn't mean erasing those stories. It meant letting them move through instead of staying stuck.

I also noticed how caring for my body changed my self-talk. I became less critical. Less demanding. More patient. I didn't rush myself through discomfort anymore. I allowed healing to be nonlinear.

That patience created trust.

And trust allowed my body to let go.

I don't believe healing is about returning to who you were before things got heavy. I believe it's about becoming someone who listens more carefully going forward.

My body didn't fail me.

It carried me through seasons I didn't yet have language for.

Healing the body that held everything wasn't about fixing damage.

It was about honoring resilience.

And once I did, my body responded — not by becoming invincible, but by becoming at ease.

That ease changed everything.

I was learning to live differently—in a body that finally believed it didn't have to stay on watch to be safe.

I wasn't just learning to think differently.

My sleep improved. My inflammation calmed. My baseline anxiety softened. My energy returned without the adrenaline spike.

Marketable

Not overnight. Not magically. But steadily.

And as I honored those cues, healing became visible.

I stopped treating stress as a sign that something was wrong with me, and started treating it as a cue: something needs attention, care, or a boundary.

Over time, my body began to respond to my mind differently—not because everything around me changed, but because the way I related to it changed.

Some days the truth was simple: I need water. I need a nap. I need to stop replaying that conversation.

Some days the truth was big: I am safe. I am loved. I am not alone.

I would sit with my journal and write a list of truths: what I knew about God, about myself, about this day.

Not the dramatic kind. The daily kind.

Truth became regulation for me.

And then I started doing something I had never done consistently before: I told the truth—out loud, on paper, and in prayer.

I started paying attention to the places stress lived in me: shoulders, jaw, gut, sleep.

I noticed how my stomach tightened when I anticipated a conversation I didn't want to have.

I noticed how quickly my heart raced when an email tone felt off.

I noticed how often I held my breath while scrolling my phone, like my lungs were bracing for bad news.

That's why healing didn't start in my mind first. It started in my body.

It carried everything—stress, grief, adrenaline, resentment, responsibility—whether I admitted it or not.

And my body obeyed those instructions the way a loyal employee obeys a demanding boss.

Strong meant: don't cry too long. Don't need too much. Don't slow down.

Strong meant: stay ready. Stay alert. Stay two steps ahead.

I didn't realize it had become a nervous-system setting.

I used to talk about "being strong" like it was a personality trait.

You are never starting from zero again. You're starting from experience.

Hold This

Your most valuable asset is not what you can produce in a crisis. It is who you are when you refuse to abandon yourself.

Try This

- What is the one sentence I want to be able to say about myself - even if everything changes?
- What would I build if I trusted my steadiness more than my speed?
- What part of my value have I been trying to prove instead of protect?

Practice: Write your one-sentence 'portable value statement' (example: 'I am steady, discerning, and creative under pressure.'). Read it daily for a week before you edit it.

Chapter 24
Letting Life Be Simple Again

"White space is not wasted space."
— Brittany P. Webb

Simplicity used to feel lazy to me.

If it wasn't complicated, I assumed it wasn't valuable.

If it wasn't hard, I assumed I hadn't earned it.

But life is not a test you pass by exhausting yourself.

Sometimes the most spiritual thing you can do is stop adding weight to what was already heavy.

For a long time, I believed complexity meant importance.

If something mattered, it should feel layered. Demanding. Slightly overwhelming. I thought meaningful lives were built by stacking responsibilities, commitments, goals, and expectations until every inch of time was accounted for.

Simple felt suspicious.

Simple felt like settling.

I didn't trust it.

But simplicity didn't arrive because I decided to want less. It arrived because I stopped needing more to feel valid.

As my life slowed and my nervous system softened, I began noticing how much effort I had been expending just to maintain unnecessary complexity. Not because life required it — but because I had learned to equate fullness with busyness.

When the noise fell away, I was surprised by how little I actually needed to feel grounded.

A slower morning.

A clear yes or no.

A conversation that didn't rush toward resolution.

An evening without obligation.

These things didn't make my life smaller.

They made it lighter.

Letting life be simple again required me to question assumptions I had never challenged. That progress had to be visible. That growth had to be dramatic. That meaning required constant motion.

I began noticing how often I complicated things out of habit.

I overexplained.

I overcommitted.

I overprepared.

Not because it was necessary — but because it was familiar.

Simplicity asked me to pause before adding. Before reacting. Before assuming something needed to be addressed immediately. Often, it didn't.

Scripture reflects this restraint beautifully:

"The Lord is my shepherd; I lack nothing."

—Psalm 23:1

Lack isn't always about resources.

Sometimes it's about restraint.

Letting life be simple meant releasing the urge to fill every space. Silence didn't need commentary. Free time didn't need productivity. Joy didn't need justification.

At first, simplicity felt almost empty.

I had been accustomed to stimulation — mentally, emotionally, logistically. Without constant input, there were moments when I didn't know what to do with myself. That discomfort tempted me to reintroduce complexity just to feel engaged again.

But I stayed.

And slowly, simplicity revealed its depth.

I noticed how much easier decisions became. How much clearer my values felt. How much energy returned when I wasn't constantly managing excess.

Simple didn't mean boring.

It meant intentional.

I chose fewer things — and chose them more fully. I stopped multitasking moments that deserved my attention. I allowed days to unfold without trying to optimize them.

This also changed how I related to success.

Success no longer meant doing the most.

It meant doing what mattered — without resentment.

I didn't need my life to look impressive.

I needed it to feel sustainable.

Simplicity also softened my expectations of myself. I stopped holding every moment to a standard. I allowed ordinary days to be enough. I let my life be lived instead of constantly evaluated.

Marketable

That shift was freeing.

I realized that much of what I once chased — clarity, peace, fulfillment — wasn't waiting in the next achievement. It was available in the quiet spaces I had been too busy to inhabit.

Jesus lived this kind of simplicity.

He withdrew often. He didn't rush. He didn't explain Himself to everyone. He focused on presence, not performance.

Simplicity, I learned, isn't a lack of ambition.

It's alignment.

Letting life be simple again didn't require me to abandon responsibility. It required me to release excess — expectations, obligations, noise — that no longer served who I was becoming.

My life didn't lose meaning.

It gained coherence.

And once I trusted simplicity, I stopped mistaking complexity for depth.

Depth lives in presence.

And presence doesn't need much to thrive.

It made me steadier.

Letting life be simple again didn't make me smaller.

But there doesn't have to be more to carry.

There will always be more to do.

Now I read it as a warning about distraction.

Jesus said Mary chose "the one thing needed" (Luke 10:42). I used to read that as a sweet story about devotion.

It's where you can enjoy your life instead of just managing it.

It's where you can feel your own needs again.

Because simple is where you can hear God again.

And I learned to bless "simple" instead of despising it.

Rhythm looks like: being fully present where I am instead of trying to be everywhere at once.

Rhythm looks like: boundaries that protect the best parts of my life.

Rhythm looks like: morning quiet, a plan for the day, time with my kids, time to breathe, time to rest.

I began building rhythms instead of reacting to demands.

Some of it was emotional: letting my feelings exist without turning them into emergency meetings.

Some of it was spiritual: praying more than ruminating. Choosing peace over proving.

Some of it was practical: fewer commitments, fewer last-minute yeses, fewer conversations that drained me.

I started paying attention to what made my days feel heavy—and what made them feel clean.

I needed a more intentional one.

And the truth is, I didn't need a more impressive life.

I was doing too much, carrying too much, explaining too much, worrying too much.

When my life got quiet, I discovered how much "noise" I had been managing—noise that looked like productivity but felt like pressure.

It's the presence of clarity.

Simplicity is not the absence of responsibility.

And the more I stopped chasing a perfect atmosphere, the more our actual atmosphere improved.

I stopped treating my house like proof that I was managing life well. I started treating it like a home people live in.

Not lowered them—simplified them.

I also simplified my standards at home.

I started leaving my phone in another room on purpose—not as a productivity hack, but as a peace decision.

I stopped "checking" things that didn't need checking.

I turned off notifications that trained my nervous system to jump.

One of the first places I practiced simplicity was my phone.

But simple taught me something complexity never could: I can be loved without being indispensable.

Complexity made me feel needed. Needed made me feel safe.

I had to grieve the version of me that equated complexity with importance.

I started treating it like a normal human day—and I learned to begin again without drama.

I stopped treating every imperfect day like evidence that I was behind.

implicity also showed up in how I talked to myself.

You are never starting from zero again. You're starting from experience.

Hold This

Marketable

Simple is not small. Simple is clear. A simple life is often the most powerful life because it makes room for what matters most.

Try This

- List three things that create noise in your week (commitments, conversations, scrolling, clutter).
- Choose one to reduce by 25% this week.
- Create one simple rhythm: a morning start, an evening wind-down, or a weekly Sabbath hour.
- When you feel rushed, repeat: "I don't have to carry everything." Simplicity isn't a finish line. It's a practice.

Chapter 25
What I No Longer Explain

"The more I explained, the more I negotiated my own boundary."
— Brittany P. Webb

I used to believe that clarity meant explaining myself until everyone agreed.

Now I believe clarity means speaking once, living it consistently, and letting people form their own opinions.

Some of the strongest moments of this season were the ones where I didn't defend my choices, didn't over-context my "no," and didn't chase understanding.

Not because I didn't care—but because I finally cared about my peace more.

There was a time when I explained everything.

My choices.

My boundaries.

My pace.

My reasons.

Not because I owed anyone an explanation — but because I was afraid of being misunderstood. Afraid that without context, my decisions might seem abrupt, selfish, or unkind. Afraid that clarity required justification.

So I talked.

I filled silence with reasoning. I softened decisions with disclaimers. I preemptively apologized for choices that didn't require apology at all.

Explanation became a form of self-protection.

But protection has a cost.

The more I explained, the less solid my decisions felt — even to me. I gave away confidence in pieces, one clarification at a time. I invited negotiation where none was necessary. I taught people that my boundaries were flexible if questioned long enough.

That wasn't honesty.

It was insecurity disguised as politeness.

As my life became quieter and more intentional, I noticed something shift. I no longer felt the reflex to justify myself. Not because I stopped caring — but because I started trusting myself.

Marketable

Trust changes how much you feel the need to explain.

I realized that explanation had been a way to manage other people's reactions. If I could help them understand why, maybe they wouldn't be disappointed. Maybe they wouldn't be upset. Maybe I wouldn't feel responsible for their discomfort.

But other people's feelings were never mine to manage.

That truth took time to settle.

When I stopped explaining, I expected conflict. I expected pushback. I expected misunderstanding.

What I got instead was clarity.

Some people adjusted immediately. Others needed time. A few didn't understand at all. And for the first time, that didn't send me spiraling.

I learned that being misunderstood is not the same as being wrong.

That distinction is freeing.

Scripture speaks directly to this kind of grounded restraint:

"Let your 'Yes' be yes, and your 'No,' no."

—Matthew 5:37

Clarity doesn't require commentary.

I stopped explaining why I needed rest.

Why I wasn't available.

Why my priorities had shifted.

I offered information when it was appropriate — not reassurance. I answered questions honestly — not defensively. I let silence do its work.

At first, this felt uncomfortable. Explanation had been my social currency. Without it, I worried I would seem cold or distant.

But something unexpected happened.

The relationships that mattered most grew steadier. Communication became cleaner. Expectations recalibrated naturally when I stopped over-functioning verbally.

I wasn't withholding.

I was trusting.

What I no longer explain are the things that don't require permission.

I don't explain why I protect my peace.

Why I say no to things that drain me.

Why I choose simplicity over busyness.

Why I don't engage every conversation that invites reaction.

These choices are not negotiable.

They are foundational.

This doesn't mean I stopped being thoughtful. It means I stopped being performative. I no longer shaped my decisions around how they might be received. I made them from alignment instead.

Alignment is quiet.

It doesn't argue.

It doesn't convince.

It doesn't defend.

It stands.

I also noticed how much energy returned when I stopped explaining myself. Conversations became lighter. My mind was clearer. I wasn't rehearsing responses or crafting explanations in advance.

I lived more in the present moment instead of preemptively managing perception.

That presence became its own explanation.

People could feel the difference.

Confidence doesn't announce itself.

It settles.

I learned that explanations are helpful when clarity is requested — but unnecessary when approval is being sought. Knowing the difference changed everything.

I no longer explain growth to people committed to my old patterns.

I let my life speak.

And my life, now, speaks clearly.

I just needed to stop betraying myself to keep the peace.

I didn't need to punish anyone.

And the people who only stay when you overgive… are telling you the truth, too.

The people who are for you don't require you to bleed to prove your intentions.

The more I practiced not explaining myself into exhaustion, the more I realized something liberating:

It's a way of staying centered when your old patterns want to sprint back into control.

It's spiritual advice.

It's nervous-system advice.

That's not just relational advice.

Scripture says it plainly: "Everyone should be quick to listen, slow to speak" (James 1:19).

Marketable

It can be wisdom.

It can be restraint.

Now I know silence can be peace.

I thought silence was punishment for a long time—an empty space I had to fill to keep things from getting awkward.

And not having the last word can be the most powerful form of self-respect.

A silence can be a boundary.

A pause can be a prayer.

Sometimes it's best to let good stuff get good stuff, and bad stuff get no stuff.

I stopped honoring disrespect with a response—in every area of my life.

I responded instead of reacting. I paused before saying yes.

I simply stopped offering my peace as a bargaining chip.

I didn't announce the change. I didn't make dramatic declarations.

So I practiced a new kind of maturity: letting my boundaries speak for themselves.

Fear that if I didn't manage the narrative, I'd lose the relationship.

Fear that I'd be judged.

Fear that I'd be misunderstood.

But overexplaining was often a form of fear.

I used to overexplain like it was courtesy. Like if I could just add enough context, people would interpret me correctly and no one would be upset.

Because I became clear.

Not because I became cold.

At some point, I stopped trying to be understood by everyone.

It's amazing how much clarity you gain when you stop explaining your boundaries to people who are committed to misunderstanding them.

Not to punish them—just to stop training them that access to me was unlimited.

Sometimes I didn't answer at all.

Sometimes I answered with one sentence.

And I practiced holding my posture anyway.

There were moments where people tested the new version of me—subtle digs, pressure, the expectation that I would bend to keep things smooth.

You don't offer five paragraphs of context to soften a two-word truth.

You don't negotiate with your own peace.

That means you don't argue with your own no.

Now I know a boundary is respected when you respect it.

I used to think a boundary had to be explained to be respected.

You are never starting from zero again. You're starting from experience.

Hold This

You don't owe everyone an explanation. You owe yourself honesty. Let your boundaries be full sentences.

Try This

- Identify one place you've been overexplaining to manage other people's reactions.
- Rewrite your boundary in one short line (example: "That doesn't work for me.").
- Practice saying it without adding extra context.
- Notice what you feel afterward—and breathe through it instead of backtracking.
  You can be kind without being consumed.

Chapter 26
The Quiet Confidence of Midlife

"Pushback doesn't always mean you're wrong."
— Brittany P. Webb

Midlife has a way of stripping away what you no longer have time to pretend about.

For me, it didn't come with a dramatic makeover or a sudden identity shift. It came with a quiet decision: I wanted my life back—my health, my energy, my presence, my peace. Over the course of this season, I lost seventy-five pounds—but the real weight that lifted was the pressure to perform for belonging.

The outside changes mattered (they were real, and hard-earned), but the deeper transformation was internal: I stopped living like I had to prove my worth and started living like I could protect it.

Midlife didn't arrive loudly for me.

There was no dramatic unraveling, no singular moment where everything fell apart and demanded attention. Instead, it arrived quietly — in awareness. In contrast. In the subtle realization that I no longer wanted to live the way I once did, even if I still could.

That was the beginning of confidence.

Not the bold, declarative kind. The quiet kind. The kind that doesn't announce itself or seek validation. The kind that comes from knowing yourself well enough to stop performing for approval.

For much of my life, confidence had been something I demonstrated. I showed it through competence. Through reliability. Through getting things done well and quickly. I proved myself through action.

That version of confidence was impressive.

It was also exhausting.

Midlife confidence didn't ask me to prove anything. It asked me to trust what I already knew. It came not from expansion, but from refinement. From releasing what no longer fit instead of acquiring something new.

I noticed how much less I needed external affirmation. Not because I stopped valuing feedback, but because my sense of self was no longer dependent on it. I didn't need constant confirmation that I was doing life "right."

I trusted my discernment.

That trust changed how I moved through the world. I spoke less urgently. I listened more fully. I made decisions without narrating the internal debate that once accompanied them.

Midlife confidence doesn't rush.

It waits.

It observes.

It chooses deliberately.

There was a time when I thought confidence meant certainty. Now I understand it means tolerance — for ambiguity, for nuance, for seasons that don't resolve quickly.

I became more comfortable saying, I don't know yet.

That comfort is powerful.

Midlife taught me that clarity doesn't always arrive on demand. Sometimes it unfolds slowly, in response to patience rather than pressure. And confidence is trusting that unfolding without forcing outcomes.

I also noticed how my relationship with time changed.

Time stopped feeling like something to outrun or maximize. It became something to inhabit. I was more aware of how quickly it moves — not in a panicked way, but in a sobering one. I stopped assuming there would always be more time later to do what mattered.

That awareness sharpened my priorities.

I spent less time on things that drained me and more time on things that nourished me. I didn't need my life to be full — I needed it to be meaningful.

Midlife confidence made me selective.

Selective with my energy.

Selective with my commitments.

Selective with my attention.

That selectivity wasn't exclusionary. It was respectful — to myself and to others. I stopped agreeing to things I couldn't show up for wholeheartedly.

Showing up halfway no longer felt acceptable.

This confidence also softened my self-judgment. I stopped critiquing myself for not being who I was ten years ago. I honored the evolution instead of mourning the shift.

I didn't need to reclaim my younger self.

I needed to integrate her.

Marketable

Midlife confidence doesn't reject the past. It absorbs it. It holds experience as wisdom instead of weight. It allows mistakes to become reference points instead of regrets.

I stopped explaining who I was becoming.

I lived it.

There was a steadiness in that — a sense of grounding that didn't depend on momentum or approval. I trusted my pace. I trusted my intuition. I trusted the quiet knowing that had replaced urgency.

This confidence didn't make me rigid.

It made me flexible.

Because when you know who you are, you're less threatened by change. You can adapt without losing yourself. You can engage without overextending. You can lead without controlling.

Midlife confidence isn't about having everything figured out.

It's about being at home in yourself — even while things are still unfolding.

And that kind of confidence doesn't need to be loud.

It's felt.

You start building a life that feels like peace.

You stop chasing a version of success that costs you your soul.

And that's what makes midlife powerful:

She's learning how to hold herself—steady, honest, and open—without giving herself away.

She doesn't need to shrink to keep other people comfortable.

She doesn't need to perform for love.

But the woman I am now doesn't need to hustle for belonging.

She was doing what she knew to do with what she knew then.

She wasn't weak.

I also felt a new kind of compassion for my younger self.

And with each step, I felt the fear lose volume.

I started treating life like a series of faithful steps.

I stopped needing every decision to be the "forever" decision.

It comes from finally trusting yourself to figure it out as you go.

Midlife confidence doesn't come from having everything figured out.

Choosing what gets your no.

Choosing what gets your yes.

Choosing what you will release.

Choosing what you will carry.

It's less about proving and more about choosing.

It's quiet confidence, not loud reinvention.

A season where you stop living for the version of you everyone expects and start listening for the version of you God is calling forward.

And it made me realize that midlife isn't a crisis—it's a crossroads.

It made me look at what I had built, what I had tolerated, what I had survived, and what I still wanted.

The honest kind.

Not the harsh kind.

Instead, it felt like a mirror.

I thought it would feel like a number—another year, another birthday, another candle.

Turning forty did something to me that I didn't expect.

I became less willing to keep paying the price of fear.

I didn't become fearless at forty.

Permission to be both soft and strong, both faithful and ambitious, both nurturing and boundaried.

Permission to change your mind.

Permission to be honest about what you want.

Permission to stop waiting for permission.

But midlife also carries a gift: permission.

For the opportunities you didn't take because you were waiting to feel "ready."

For the versions of yourself you abandoned to keep things working.

For the years you spent overgiving.

It's grief for time.

It's not grief for someone who died.

There's a kind of midlife grief that doesn't always get named.

You are never starting from zero again. You're starting from experience.

Hold This

Midlife isn't the end of your story. It's the moment you stop living on autopilot and start choosing what you actually want to carry forward.

Try This

- Write: "I am not too late to _____." Fill it in with something true.
- Name one thing your younger self needed that you can give yourself now.
- Choose one "quiet confidence" action: wear what you love, speak up once, rest without guilt, or say no without explaining.
- Thank God for the wisdom you earned the hard way.

Confidence grows when you keep showing up as the same person in private and in public.

Chapter 27
The Life I'm Building Now

"Being misunderstood is sometimes the price of being honest."
— Brittany P. Webb

Starting over is humbling.

It's also holy, if you let it be.

When you build again from scratch, you learn quickly what you're actually made of—and what you were only carrying because you thought you had to.

I didn't rebuild to impress anyone.

I rebuilt to be free.

And that difference changed everything about what I was willing to do— and what I was no longer willing to tolerate.

The life I'm building now doesn't look the way I once imagined it would.

It's quieter.

Less crowded.

Less performative.

And somehow, more honest.

For a long time, I lived oriented toward the next version of myself. The next milestone. The next achievement that would signal arrival. Life felt like something I was moving toward rather than something I was inhabiting.

That orientation shaped everything.

I made decisions based on future payoff. I tolerated discomfort because it felt temporary. I postponed rest, joy, and ease because they could wait until later.

Later always felt just close enough to justify pushing through.

Now looks different.

I'm no longer building toward a finish line. I'm building toward alignment. Toward a life that fits the person I am becoming instead of the person I once needed to be.

This life isn't defined by certainty.

It's defined by intention.

I choose my pace now. I choose how full my days feel. I choose how much energy I give and where I give it. That choice doesn't come from control — it comes from awareness.

Marketable

I know what depletion feels like.

I know what misalignment costs.

I know what happens when I ignore my body, my intuition, my faith.

Those experiences didn't break me.

They informed me.

The life I'm building now has margin.

Not because I do less, but because I do differently. I leave space in my days for rest without guilt. For creativity without outcome. For conversation without agenda.

Margin isn't wasted time.

It's where life happens.

I've also stopped waiting for permission to enjoy the present. I no longer assume joy needs to be justified by productivity. I let moments be meaningful without turning them into proof of anything.

That shift has changed how I work.

I'm more focused. More thoughtful. Less reactive. I trust my instincts instead of overriding them. I allow projects to evolve instead of forcing momentum. I value depth over volume.

This way of working doesn't impress everyone.

It doesn't need to.

I'm building something sustainable — not just professionally, but personally. I want the work I do to coexist with my life, not compete with it. I want success to feel integrated, not extractive.

The life I'm building now also holds faith differently.

Faith is no longer a tool I use to endure pressure. It's the foundation that keeps me oriented when things feel uncertain. I don't ask it to explain everything. I trust it to anchor me.

That trust allows me to live with unanswered questions without rushing toward resolution.

I don't need clarity immediately.

I need presence.

This life also reflects a different relationship with ambition.

I'm still ambitious — but not at the cost of myself. I care deeply about what I build. I take responsibility seriously. I pursue excellence.

But I no longer sacrifice peace to prove worth.

That trade no longer makes sense to me.

The life I'm building now is intentional, not perfect. There are days when old habits surface. When urgency tries to reclaim space. When I feel the pull to overextend.

But now, I notice.

And noticing gives me choice.

Choice is what defines this season.

I'm choosing honesty over optics.

Presence over performance.

Sustainability over speed.

I'm choosing a life that doesn't require recovery from itself.

This isn't a declaration of arrival.

It's a commitment to continue.

To stay awake.

To listen.

To adjust when necessary.

The life I'm building now doesn't need to be defended or explained.

It just needs to be lived.

And living it — fully, attentively, without apology — feels like the truest measure of success I've known.

A whole one.

Not a perfect life.

That's what I want for you too.

And I'm building a life that can hold all of it—faith, family, work, creativity, rest—without demanding that any one part of me disappear.

But as an internal certainty: I know what I bring. I know what I've built. I know what I survived. I know what I'm becoming.

Not as a gold star from corporate culture.

Not as approval from a past employer.

The irony is that the more I stopped chasing "marketability," the more it showed up.

And a commitment to do it without losing myself again.

An obsession with helping people stop drowning in what could be solved with clarity.

My ecosystem has a structure now—B Creative Systems, Prompt Therapy™, Bline™—but underneath all of it is something simpler:

And I started making room for joy inside the work, not just after it.

I started creating offers that help people get organized, automated, and grounded—without turning their lives into a performance.

Marketable

I started designing systems that protect peace, not just productivity.

But as I healed, my building changed.

When I believed I had to earn worth, I built out of proving.

When I believed I had to earn safety, I built out of control.

When I believed I had to earn love, I built out of overgiving.

Because the way you build is always influenced by who you believe you are.

Now I know they're braided together.

I used to separate "healing" and "work" like they were two different lanes.

But it also looks like a quieter home, a more regulated nervous system, and a woman who no longer needs to be in crisis to feel alive.

It looks like books and systems and brands, yes.

The life I'm building now doesn't fit in one box.

And I didn't heal just to repeat the same pattern with a prettier logo.

If my work ever requires me to lose myself again, it isn't success. It's a repeat.

The goal is a life that feels true—and a business that supports it.

The goal isn't a brand that looks impressive.

Information I can learn from without collapsing.

When I build out of alignment, setbacks feel like information.

When I built out of proving, setbacks felt like identity threats.

It also changes how you recover from setbacks.

It changes the offers you create, the clients you take, the pace you keep, and the way you measure success.

That question changes everything.

But "How do I stay whole while I build?"

Not "How do I scale?" first.

I'm building with a different question now.

You are never starting from zero again. You're starting from experience.

Hold This

A whole life isn't built by doing more. It's built by aligning what you do with who you are becoming—so your work, faith, and family reinforce each other instead of competing.

Try This

- Write down the five words you want your life to feel like in this season (example: steady, joyful, clear, faithful, free).
- Audit your calendar: what supports those words, and what fights them?
- Pick one change you can make this week that matches your desired feel.
- Pray over the work you're building and ask for peace to lead the plan.
  If peace leaves when you "succeed," that version of success is too expensive.

Chapter 28
What I Would Tell the Woman Behind Me

"Marketable isn't perfect. It's trusted."
— Brittany P. Webb

If I could sit across from her—coffee between us, her shoulders still tense from carrying too much—I wouldn't start with advice.

I would start with permission.

Permission to breathe.

Permission to stop proving.

Permission to be loved without constantly being useful.

And then, gently, I would remind her: the version of her that survives is not the final version. She is allowed to become.

I would tell her to slow down — not because she's doing it wrong, but because she's doing too much alone.

I would tell her that the exhaustion she feels isn't a personal failure. It's a signal. One she's been taught to override, to work through, to minimize because everyone depends on her strength.

I would tell her that strength isn't what's being asked of her next.

Honesty is.

I would tell her that the version of herself she's trying to maintain is not the one she has to protect forever. That it's okay to let seasons end. That outgrowing old rhythms doesn't mean she wasted the years she lived inside them.

I would tell her that nothing is wrong because things feel heavy.

They feel heavy because she's carrying more than was meant to be carried by one person.

I would tell her that rest won't come all at once. That peace will arrive in fragments before it arrives in fullness. That neutrality is not emptiness — it's recovery.

I would tell her not to rush joy.

Joy doesn't reappear the way adrenaline does. It doesn't announce itself. It doesn't demand attention. It shows up quietly and asks permission to stay.

I would tell her that she doesn't need to explain herself as much as she thinks. That the people meant to grow with her will adjust. That being misunderstood for a season is not the same as being alone.

I would tell her that boundaries will feel uncomfortable at first — not because they're wrong, but because they interrupt patterns she's been living inside for years.

I would tell her that saying no doesn't make her unkind.

It makes her honest.

I would tell her that she is allowed to choose a life that fits her nervous system, her faith, her body, and her season — even if it doesn't match the expectations that once guided her.

I would tell her that she doesn't need to burn everything down to begin again. That sometimes the bravest thing she can do is stay — and do things differently.

I would tell her that clarity will come, but not on demand. That she can trust what's unfolding even when it feels slow. That urgency is not the same as importance.

I would tell her that she doesn't have to become someone new.

She has to come back to herself.

I would tell her that there will be moments when she doubts her decision to stop, to pause, to choose differently. That old patterns will call her back with familiar language — productivity, usefulness, responsibility.

I would tell her that familiarity does not equal truth.

I would tell her that her body will soften before her mind fully trusts the change. That healing will show up in unexpected ways — deeper sleep, quieter thoughts, laughter she doesn't brace for.

I would tell her that her faith will feel different, and that difference is not loss. That belief without performance is steadier than belief built on effort.

I would tell her that the life she's afraid to choose is often the one that will hold her best.

I would tell her that nothing she is becoming will betray the woman she's been. That every version of her carried something forward — even the tired ones.

And most of all, I would tell her this:

You are not behind.

You are arriving — slowly, honestly, and in your own time.

And the life waiting for you does not require you to disappear to earn it.

You are building from experience.

You are not starting from scratch.

You are not too late.

You are not behind.

Marketable

And most of all, I'd tell you this:

Sometimes the strongest move is to take your foot off the pedals and let the weight of what's real bring you back to steady.

Like hydroplaning: sometimes the strongest move isn't to slam the brakes or overcorrect.

Healing is repetition—choosing the new response again and again until it becomes your reflex.

That's normal.

There will be days you feel brave and days you feel like you lost progress.

I'd also tell you that healing isn't a straight line.

Sometimes you start over by letting God fight a battle you keep trying to win with words.

Sometimes you start over by letting people be disappointed and choosing peace anyway.

Sometimes you start over by saying no without explaining.

Sometimes you start over by telling the truth for the first time.

You don't have to burn everything down to start over.

And I'd tell you that reinvention doesn't have to be loud to be real.

I'd tell you that prayer is not a last resort. It's a strategy.

I'd tell you that silence is not punishment. It's space.

I'd tell you that boundaries will trigger pushback—and that pushback is often proof you needed the boundary.

I'd tell you that being the reliable one is not the same as being the loved one.

I'd tell you that you don't have to earn rest with exhaustion.

I'd tell you that your sensitivity is not a flaw. It's information.

If you were a few steps behind me on this road, I'd want to sit you down with a cup of coffee and tell you the things I didn't learn fast enough.

And once your body learns that, your life will follow.

You are learning what safety actually feels like.

If you're in the messy middle, I want you to hear me: you are not failing.

And you can rebuild without hating your past self for surviving the only way she knew how.

You can love someone and still choose distance.

You can forgive and still require change.

I'd remind you that you can be both tender and firm.

I'd tell you to stop calling your boundaries "mean."

I'd tell you to stop calling your desire for peace "lazy."

I would tell you to stop calling your sensitivity "too much."

Take the step while you're shaky. God can steady you mid-step.

Confidence is often the result, not the prerequisite.

If you're waiting to feel confident before you act, you may be waiting forever.

You are never starting from zero again. You're starting from experience.

Hold This

You don't need a dramatic restart to begin again. You need one honest decision, repeated until it becomes your new normal.

Try This

- Write a short note to the version of you that still thinks she has to earn love.
- List three boundaries you're afraid to set—and the cost of not setting them.
- Choose one small brave action for today (one conversation, one no, one pause, one prayer).
- End the day by naming one way you showed up for yourself.
  Your next step doesn't have to be loud. It just has to be true.

Chapter 29
The Woman Who Holds Herself

"Freedom is light, but it still asks for something."
— Brittany P. Webb

There was a time when I believed holding everything together was the highest form of strength.

I thought resilience meant endurance.

That love meant availability.

That faith meant perseverance at any cost.

So I held it all — the schedules, the emotions, the expectations, the outcomes. I held space for others before I learned how to hold myself.

What I didn't know then was that holding everything eventually requires something to give.

And what finally gave was not my life — but my illusion of control over it.

The woman who holds herself does not arrive suddenly. She is revealed gradually, through pauses she once avoided and questions she once silenced. She appears when the woman who held everything realizes that strength without care becomes strain.

Holding oneself is different.

It requires listening instead of bracing.

Discernment instead of urgency.

Presence instead of performance.

It asks a woman to stay with herself — even when answers are slow, even when clarity takes time, even when the world does not immediately understand the change.

The woman who holds herself still shows up.

She loves deeply.

She works honestly.

She gives generously.

But she no longer gives at the expense of her own center.

She understands that boundaries are not walls — they are supports. That rest is not retreat — it is regulation. That peace is not something earned after exhaustion — it is something chosen along the way.

She no longer confuses being needed with being valued.

She knows the difference now.

Holding herself means trusting her body when it signals fatigue instead of overriding it. It means honoring her intuition without demanding proof. It means letting faith be a refuge instead of a requirement.

It means allowing silence to be neutral — even kind.

This woman is not hardened by what she's lived.

She is softened.

She carries wisdom without bitterness. She speaks with restraint because she no longer needs to convince. She chooses carefully because she understands the cost of overextension.

She has learned that not every season requires explanation.

Some seasons only require honesty.

The woman who holds herself understands that growth does not mean constant expansion. Sometimes it means consolidation. Integration. Letting what matters settle into place.

She no longer measures her life by output alone.

She measures it by alignment.

By whether her days feel inhabitable.

By whether her relationships feel mutual.

By whether her faith feels grounding instead of demanding.

She trusts herself to know when to move — and when to be still.

This woman does not disappear from her life to make it work.

She stays.

She stays present.

She stays attentive.

She stays rooted.

And because she does, everything else finds its proper weight.

This book is not about leaving everything behind.

It is about returning — to self, to faith, to a life that no longer requires self-erasure to sustain it.

The woman who once held everything has not failed.

She has evolved.

She has learned that holding herself is not selfish — it is essential. That peace is not passive — it is practiced. That strength is not proven by endurance alone — but by discernment.

And now, she moves forward differently.

Not because life is easy.

Not because uncertainty is gone.

Marketable

But because she is no longer carrying it all alone.
She holds herself.
And that is enough.

You are never starting from zero again. You're starting from experience.

Hold This

Integration is when your life stops needing to look impressive to feel aligned.

Try This

- What would change if I let 'peace' be my compass?
- What am I doing to look okay that is costing me peace?
- Where am I chasing validation instead of alignment?

Practice: Choose one area (work, relationships, body, faith). Ask: 'What is the most peaceful next step that still honors my responsibility?' Do that.

Chapter 30
What Grew in the Quiet

"You will recognize them by their fruit." (Matthew 7:16)

At first, the quiet felt like punishment.

Not because I was doing nothing — but because I wasn't doing what I was trained to do: prove. Produce. Perform. Stay needed. Stay chosen.

In that season, I didn't have the comfort of a title or the certainty of a next step. I had legal constraints I wouldn't break, a story I wouldn't broadcast, and a future I couldn't control. What I did have was time — and a decision.

I could fill the space with panic, noise, and rumination. Or I could treat the space like holy ground and build what I could from the inside out.

I didn't always choose well at first. Some mornings were steady. Some were shaky. I felt peace and fear in the same hour. But little by little, the quiet stopped being empty and started being fertile.

Here is what grew there — not as a flex, and not as a scoreboard — but as proof that your value does not disappear when a system turns away from you. Sometimes, the quiet is where God reintroduces you to yourself.

- I wrote. Not because I had a perfectly mapped plan, but because truth needed somewhere to go. Words became a way to steady my mind and reclaim my voice.
- I built a rebranded home for my work — a website that reflected the full ecosystem I was becoming, not just the role I had once held.
- I created Prompt Therapy™ — not as a replacement for professional care, but as a structured reflective practice with AI that helped me name what I felt, regulate my nervous system, close loops, and move forward without abandoning myself.
- I started B Creative Systems™ — the place where experience, strategy, and soul could coexist — and where I could serve without disappearing.
- I mapped the frameworks that added structure to my vision: the 12.5 Signature Marketing System™ and B10 Core Automation™ Method, building a repeatable way to help people create digital marketing clarity.
- I began developing Bline™ — a branded streamlined backend marketing system in motion — because I could see the gap between what

Marketable

businesses think they need, what they actually need to sustain growth, and how they achieve growth through empowerment and execution.

- I created merchandise and tangible reminders, not because I needed "stuff," but because I wanted women to have language they could wear — a small way to carry truth into ordinary days.
- And, in time, independent signals followed — including a Google Knowledge Panel — a quiet reminder that you can become findable without being endorsed by the people who once held the microphone.

The point isn't that you have to do all of that. When I was interviewing and being told I was too ambitious for roles, I chose to continue to move towards where I wanted to be. Staying sharp. Up to date. Relevant. On-trend. With Marketability. Whether someone else said it, or not.

The point is that when the external validation disappears, you are still here. You still have mind, faith, skill, creativity, discernment, and the ability to rebuild from integrity.

If you are in a quiet season right now — a waiting season, a rebuilding season, a season where you can't talk about everything and you can't control what's next — I want you to hear this clearly:

Quiet does not mean you are behind. Quiet can be where you recover your MVP asset.

And when you step forward again, you won't be asking the world to tell you who you are. You'll already know.

I recovered the MVP asset: me.

Hold This

Quiet seasons are not blank spaces. They are proving grounds.

If you can't control the outcome right now, you can still control the soil: what you feed your mind, what you practice, what you build, and what you refuse to compromise.

Fruit doesn't always grow in public. Sometimes it grows where no one claps—where only God sees.

Try This

The Quiet Season Inventory (10 minutes):

1.   Write three lists:

What I'm not allowed to do right now:
(legal constraints, waiting, silence, limitations)

What I can do right now:
(one skill, one relationship, one piece of progress)

What is growing in me right now:
(peace, discipline, clarity, courage, self-trust, faith, creativity)

2.   Choose one daily "fruit practice" for the next 7 days:

- 10 minutes of writing
- 10 minutes of learning
- 10 minutes of movement
- 10 minutes of prayer (before you think/talk about it)
- one small build step (a page, a plan, a pitch, a product)

3.   End each day with this sentence:

"Today, I didn't waste the quiet. I worked the soil.

Final Chapter
The Asset I Didn't Know I Was

"Marketable isn't being chosen by a system. It's being steady without one."
— Brittany P. Webb

I thought I was starting over.

That's how it looked from the outside—leaving what was familiar, releasing the identity that had been reinforced by productivity and performance, stepping into uncertainty without a neatly labeled next step. Starting over carries a certain humility. It suggests loss. Risk. A return to zero.

But I wasn't starting from nothing.

I was starting from myself.

For a long time, I believed my value lived outside of me—in what I produced, how available I was, how well I held everything together. I measured worth in output and reliability. I thought security came from being indispensable.

What I didn't realize was that in all of that building, striving, and surviving, something far more durable had been forming.

Me.

Not the version of me defined by titles or roles. Not the one praised for endurance or rewarded for compliance. But the version forged through awareness, restraint, discernment, faith, and hard-earned self-trust.

That was the asset.

Marketable was never about becoming something new. It was about becoming transferable without losing myself. It was about discovering that the most valuable thing I carried into every room, every season, every rebuild—was not my résumé, my output, or my capacity to overfunction.

It was my clarity.

My ability to regulate instead of react.

My capacity to pause instead of perform.

My discernment about what is mine to carry—and what is not.

My steadiness in uncertainty.

My faith when outcomes are unknown.

Those qualities don't disappear when jobs end, systems shift, or identities evolve. They compound.

That's what makes them marketable.

Not in a transactional sense—but in a deeply human one.

I no longer need to prove my value by showing how much I can hold. I know my value because I know who I am when I stop holding everything. I've learned that peace is not a byproduct of success—it's a prerequisite for sustainability. That clarity outlasts roles. That self-trust is portable. That faith doesn't require certainty to be strong.

Everything I thought I lost when I stepped back—structure, momentum, recognition—made room for something I could finally keep.

Myself.

And once you reclaim that asset, you realize something powerful:

You are never starting over from zero again.

You are starting from wisdom.

From experience.

From alignment.

From a version of yourself that can enter any future without abandoning who you've become.

That is Marketable.

Not because the world demands it.

But because it lasts.

Meet the Author

Brittany P. Webb is an author, creator, and builder with a passion for intentional growth and sharing a message of hope and faith-rooted clarity for those in need—especially women who've carried too much for too long.

As a mother of three and a wife, Brittany stepped away from a corporate season that shaped her—and shook her—and entered what looked like "starting over," but became something else entirely: a quiet, holy, resilient rebuild. Not a reinvention for applause, but a return to herself—aligned, peaceful, and without needing a title to validate her worth.

In one year, she authored and published five books, including Momma Knows Best, The Uncommon AffAIr, Prompt Therapy: The Uncommon AffAIr with AI, The Uncommon AffAIr with AI Prompt Therapy Workbook, and MarketABLE. She also offers a digital download of her foundational Prompt Therapy™ Self-Starter Guide. Together, these are a prime example of what she refers to as AIfficiency™. Her work blends story, scripture, faith and inspiration, emotional intelligence, and practical self-leadership—written to encourage women who are capable on the outside, but tired of surviving on the inside.

Brittany is the creator of Prompt Therapy™ (a structured reflective practice with AI that helps people process honestly and move forward with clarity) and the founder of B Creative Systems™, where strategy and soul can coexist in business through marketing and digital foundations.

Connect with Brittany P. Webb at brittanypwebb.com

www.ingramcontent.com/pod-product-compliance
Lightning Source LLC
Chambersburg PA
CBHW070923130626
46555CB00001B/253